info
The complete

Distributed by:

UK
A.A. Publishing
(A Division of the
Automobile Association)
Fanum House
Basingstoke
Hampshire RG21 2EA

Australia
Gordon & Gotch Ltd,
25-37 Huntingdale Road,
Burwood
Victoria 3125

First published and produced
in Australia in 1990 by:

T.P. Books & Print Pty Ltd
Suite 13, 3 Moore Lane
Harbord Village
Harbord NSW 2096

In Association with:

Tourist Publications
6 Pilliou Street
Koliatsou Square
112 55 Athens, Greece

© Copyright Tourist Publications 1990

Editorial Directors:	L. Starr
	Y. Skordilis
Author:	Kerry & Geoff Kenihan
Typography:	M. Roetman
Design:	C. Mills
Layout:	C. Mills
Photosetting:	Deblaere Typesetting Pty Ltd
Photographs:	Kerry Kenihan
	Gov. of India Tourist Office
	Benanji Pty Ltd
Maps:	Judy Trim

Printed in Australia

ISBN 1 872163 20 3

All rights reserved. No part of this book may be reproduced or transmitted in any form or by any means, electronic or mechanical, including photocopying, recording or by any information storage and retrieval system, without written permission from the publisher.

Due to the wealth of information available, it has been necessary to be selective. Sufficient detail is given to allow the visitor to make choices depending on personal taste, and the information has been carefully checked. However, errors creep in and changes will occur. We hope you will forgive the errors and omissions and find this book a helpful companion.

ABOUT THIS GUIDE

Elegant, modern, yet resplendent with palaces, temples and forts testifying to a turbulent past, Delhi, India's capital will be discovered as a city of gardens, and a place of the old and the new through this guide.

The guide will also take you on a romantic visit to fabled Kashmir of the Himalayas and houseboats for a change of pace and atmosphere.

Part I offers information of Delhi and India's history, religions, culture, geology, flora, fauna and languages.etc

Part II explores the varied streets of Old and New Delhi and takes you on a relaxed flight into fantasy in the vale of Kashmir before a glimpse of the Taj Mahal at Agra.

Part III includes hints on gaining accommodation and a comprehensive list of what is available.

Part IV presents the practicalities, how to get around, where to eat and what, best shopping and where to go for assistance...... and more.

Part V will be invaluable to business travellers but vacationers should find this section of interest also.

Delhi is a right royal city and we hope you will enjoy its pageantry and paradoxes.

Acknowledgements

We are indebted to the **personnel** of the **Government of India Tourist Office, Sydney**, also **Delhi** for their support and interest, **Air India** for international transport to and from India and to the **staff of Air India, Adelaide**, South Australia for their knowledge and enthusiasm. We are also grateful to **Australian Airlines** for authors' connecting flights in their home country.

Table of Contents

PART I - INDIA AND HER PEOPLE
- Geology and Geography 10
- Climate 11
- Flora and Fauna 12
- Government 14
- Education 16
- Commerce and Industry 16
- Religions 17
- The People of India 27
- Meeting People 28
- Indian Languages 30
- History and Culture 32
- India's Glorious Architecture 43

PART II - SIGHTSEEING
DELHI, 3000 YEARS OF HISTORY 51
GRACE OF EMPIRES 52
OLD DELHI, DEFENCES AND DELIGHTS 53
- The Red Fort 53
- Fort Museums 55
- Son Et Lumiere 56
- Jama Masjid 56
- Chandi Chowk 57
- Ashoka's Pillar 58
- Connaught Palace 58
- Jantar Mantar Observatory 60
- Raj Ghat 61
- Laxshmi Narayan Temple 62
- Mahatma Gandi Memorial Museum 62
- Feroz Shah Kotla Ashoka's Pillar 62
- International Dolls Museum 63
- Khuni Darwaza (Kabuli) 64
- Crafts Museum 65
- Purana Quila (Old Fort) 65
- Delhi Zoo 66
- Hymayan's Tomb 66
- Hazrat Nizamuddin Aulia 67
- Tibet House 68
- Lodi Gardens 68
- Safdarjang's Tomb 68
- India Gate 70
- Raj Path, In Its Steps 70
- Vigyan Bhavan 70
- The National Museum 71

Parliament House	71
The Secretarial Complex	71
Rashtrapati Bhavan	72
Nehru Memorial Museum	72
Rail Transport Museum	74
Diplomatic Enclave	75
The Qutab Minar	76
Quwwat-ul-Islam Mosque	76
The Iron Pillar	76
Hauz Khas	78
Qutab Minar Complex	79
Tughlakabad	80
KASHMIR	80
Vales of Awesome Beauty	80
Shankracharya Temple	84
Nishat Bagh (Gardens)	85
Shalimar Bagh (Gardens)	85
Harwan	85
Naseem Bagh (Gardens)	85
Hazratbal Mosque	86
Cheshma Shahi	87
Pari Mahal	87
Shri Pratap Singh Museum	87
Shah Hamdan Mosque	88
Pather Masjid	88
Jami Masjid	88
Hari Parbat Fort	88
AGRA	92
The Taj and Fatehpursikri	92
The Red Fort	92
The Taj Mahal	93
Itmad-ud-Daulah's Tomb	93
Fatehpursikri	93
The Palace on Wheels	96

PART III - HOTELS 103
   Camping 104
   Hotels Delhi 104
   Hotels Srinagar 110

PART IV - PRACTICAL INFORMATION
   A-Z Summary 114

PART V - BUSINESS GUIDE 181

MAPS
   Town Plan 98
   India 193

INDEX 194

PART I
General Introduction

INDIA AND HER PEOPLE

MOTHER INDIA AND HER CHILDREN

India is such a vast country - by area, population, history and culture that one could spend a lifetime attempting to discover all of its fascinating facets.

However, even a brief experience of the colourful nation's culture, religion, ancient and modern architecture, music, dance, painting and sculpture, fairs and festivals, traditional crafts and its tempting cuisines, will weave a spell that will never be broken. India's scenery is as diverse as it is dramatic, from the towering, snow-capped Himalayas descending into desert, rolling plains, tropical forests and beaches washed by three seas.

Its wildlife will stir the imagination of anyone who has ever read the stories of Indian-born English author and poet, Rudyard Kipling, or any, who as a child, was captivated by pictures of panthers, tigers, elephants and monkeys.

India is unlike many other countries which have been progressively modernized in the second half of the 20th century. While its capital city, Delhi offers sophistication, deluxe facilities and the high life to those who seek it, there are also smaller cities, towns and villages close by which have stood still in time. Therefore, in India, the visitor is presented with rare opportunity - to step into a mystic, living past.

International tourism has come late to India. It is to the traveller's advantage that this vast sub-continent below Asia is blooming in an era of world tourism. India has not made the mistake of some other nations where great monuments to past glories have been torn down to make way for modern developments or even relocated far away from their original sites. India's past still lives as vibrantly as its diverse peoples with their many and varied religions and the tourist industry is serving to maintain the nation's heritage. In practical terms, one can live the past - in a former Maharajah's palace, a Hill Station resort or a luxurious houseboat, any of which are living echoes of the great and glorious British Raj.

One can also travel through seven cities on a royal vintage train - The Palace Train out of Delhi - created for the princely rulers and British viceroys more than 80 years ago. Luxury modern hotels and beach resorts are the equal to the world's best. This surprises some new visitors who read of India being a third world country.

Away from the exotic, India provides exciting opportunities for adventure and sport, from skiing, mountain climbing, white water river rafting to hang gliding or joining a camel safari. Yet, in addition, the traveller in India will also meet the people who still hold sacred their life-giving rivers, worship the aimless cow and devoutly believe that their sins will be absolved when they wash their bodies in the holy River Ganges. The people regard their India as a cohesive whole yet the foreigner invariably experiences it as a series of fascinating places which developed in different centuries under several faiths and races.

India's cosmopolitanism, its industry and the plight of its poor are easy to see. But its complexities and its paradoxes of old and new, rich and poor all blend to weave a tapestry that is an enigma. The temptation to understand is irresistable to the traveller.

GEOLOGY AND GEOGRAPHY

Geologically, India is divided into three parts, the Himalayas, the Indo-Gangetic Plain and the Deccan Peninsula.

The great Himalayas in the north were once covered by sea, and were formed by layer upon layer of marine deposits. The 1,500-mile long mountain chain has roughly five longtitudinal divisions and it is separated from the Tibetan Plateau by the valleys of the Upper Indus and Brahmaputra rivers. Created in the Tertiary Age, there are more than 60 peaks rising above 24,000 feet, culminating in the world's highest mountain - Everest which is in Nepal and Tibet. The lesser Himalayas are a number of ranges reaching heights of 12,000 feet, enclosing valleys such as the Vale of Kashmir.

The Indo-Gangetic Plain is the geological depression between the folding of the Himalayas and the peninsula structure of India. In the eastern sections of the plain, deposits are chiefly alluvial while in the west, windblown material is significant. It consists of sands and muds. Nearly 25 per cent of India is drained by the River Ganges, known as the Mother of India.

The geological history of the Deccan Peninsula of India is extremely complicated. Its rivers are shorter and drain far less areas than the three great systems of the north - the Ganges, the Indus and the Brahmaputra.

Roughly triangularly shaped, India is the world's seventh largest country and is bordered by Pakistan in the north east, China to the north west and east, Nepal, Tibet, Bhutan and Bangladesh and Burma to the east. India's most southerly point, Cape Comorin, is on the eighth degree of latitude and the nation's most northerly frontier

India and Her People

lies on the 37th. India has a land area slightly in excess of 1,260,000 square miles. Its coastline is washed by the Arabian Sea in the west and the Bay of Bengal in the east. The Indian Ocean lies to the south. The nation is divided close to its southern tip from the independent island of Sri Lanka just 30 miles across the Palk Straits at the nearest point.

Presidential Palace

CLIMATE

There are three main seasons in India - summer, winter and the time of the monsoon. The weather is generally pleasant throughout the winter months between November and March although in the northern plains, night temperatures can be quite cold and, in the mountains, drop below freezing point. In Kashmir and the Himalayas, it is extremely cold under snow. Winter time in the south is warm without any real cold being experienced.

The summer months between April and June are hot throughout India with the exception of the Himalayan foothills which are balmy by day and a little crisp at night. When temperatures soar, particularly in the south, the British-created hill stations provide cool retreats as does Kashmir, north of Delhi.

Summer is followed by the breaking of the south west monsoon along the west coast and the rains extend gradually across the country. Apart from the south east parts of India, the greatest part of the annual rainfall is received between the end of June to the end of September. The south east area is influenced by the north east monsoon when annual rainfall is mostly experienced between mid-October and the end of December. Dry summer in Delhi can be extremely hot. Best time to visit is between mid-September and March when mostly the days are crisp, fine and sunny while evenings are nicely cool. The time of the monsoon is also a pleasant season in which to visit the capital.

FLORA AND FAUNA

While the sub-continent of India has no flora naturally unique to its area, it boasts a huge diversity of trees, shrubs and flowers ranging from the southern tropical zones to the mid- temperate areas of the north. The country can be divided into three main botanical sections - Himalayan, western and eastern.

The Himalayan region abounds with conifers, poplar, plane and oak trees with colourful rhododendrons and magnolias among many other flowers. Tree growth is relatively rare and stunted in the Indus and Gangetic Plain regions although the deltas of both the Indus and the Ganges have dense, evergreen forests of trees and shrubs in which the mangrove is predominant.

There is also the spreading, significant banyun tree under which Lord Buddha preached his first sermon. Since, it has always represented reflection and spirituality. Thick forests still remain in the hilly sections of the south. Along the south east coast, particularly Goa where bougainvillea is brilliant in its variety of colours and profusion, there is tropical growth galore. India's main cultivated plants include rice, wheat, tea, coffee, fruit trees and, in the south, the coconut palm.

The deepest of links has always existed between the races of India and their natural environment. Perhaps nowhere is this more deeply rooted than in the relationship between man and the wildlife's vast plains and forests. This union with nature originates in antiquity when the holymen, who claimed perception of a world beyond normal human experience, made ecstatic journeys on the backs of tigers. Animals were the vehicles on which the gods of India moved - the swan, the peacock, the snake, the bull, the monkey and the elephant, to name a few.

Today India is in the forefront of the nations of the world in preserving its natural heritage of fauna. India sees its

India and Her People

wildlife as a natural treasure and the country abounds with wildlife reserves sheltering and preserving more than 500 species of mammals and countless birds and reptiles.

The Western Himalayas are the last refuge of the Kashmir stag, a sub-species of the red deer and they also harbour a diversity of natural fauna including the snow leopard, the black and brown bear, the Ibex, a type of wild goat, and the musk deer.

The forest area of the Himalayan foothills is one of the main habitats of the tiger. There are also leopards, elephants and deer.

These can be seen in the **Corbett National Park** which is threaded by the **Ramganga river**. Here, there are two types of crocodile. Monkeys also inhabit the north.

In the arid **state of Rajasthan** is the Ghana waterbird sanctuary at Bharatpur which has several hundred species of resident and migratory visitors. In Rajasthan can also be found (mainly in national parks,) rugged species of deer, tigers and in India's only desert, the **Barmer-Jaisalmer**, are desert wolf, cat and fox.

The central western State of Gujarat is refuge to the Asiatic lion, leopards and antelopes. It has cranes and flamingoes on its **Lake Nalsarovar** and the adjoining central State of Madhya Prudesh is the heart of tiger country in the nation's core. The **Kanha National Park** has also wild dog, deer and the area is known as Kipling Country because the famous Jungle Books were set here.

Green Delhi

Elephant, gaur, wild dog, mouse deer, sloth bears and, occasionally, giant squirrels can be found in the south, particularly at Karnatal's Bandipur Tiger Reserve and Nagarhole. Kaziranga National Park, on the Brahmaputra's banks in Assam in the east, is home to the one-horned rhinoceros and the Indian wild buffalo. In Assam's thick, evergreen forests are leopards.

Cat bears and red pandas live in the eastern Himalaya's temperate forests. India also has wolves and panthers which may be seen by the visitor who has travelled the few kilometres from Bombay to Sanjay Gandhi National Park and the Kanheri Caves. Here, they roam but mostly at night.

Birds in India include parrots, four types of vulture, hawks, falcons, kingfishers, kites, herons, mynah birds and game birds are snipe, pigeons, partridges, quail and red jungle fowl.

In rural areas, snakes intrude into gardens and sometimes dwellings, mostly in the rainy season. There is the Russelian snake and also cobra which you'll see being charmed in the streets of Bombay, Delhi and some other cities. The Russelian snake has a lethal bite as does the small krait.

Fish include trout, kingfish (excellent eating in Goa, in particular,) and carp. There are also crayfish, oysters, mussels and prawns. The cow, of course, is sacred. Dogs roam as strays or are kept as pets and a few cats can be seen around bazaars and markets where they keep the mouse population down. There are also water buffalo, sheep and goats.

GOVERNMENT

India is a Federal Republic firmly based on the inheritance of the British Westminster system of parliamentary democracy but with some relatively recent changes that are similar to the government of the United States.

There is a balance of administration and power between the central government in the Federal Capital of Delhi and 25 State governments. There are also seven territories in India which are administered by the central government. This system was seen by the architects of independent India as the best way of serving the interests of the people and has been enshrined in the nation's Constitution.

The central government has two parliamentary houses, the lower house being the **Lok Sabha** or House of the People and an upper chamber called **Rajya Sabha** or the Council of States. There is universal adult franchise in India

India and Her People

Garden of Presidential Palace

and the people elect nearly 500 members to the Lok Sabha while the Council of States has about 250 representatives. Both houses of parliament, together with the State Parliaments, are involved in electing the president of the nation but the office of president is more symbolic as a head of State with true power vested in the Prime Minister.

Since 1952, elections for the House of the People have been held approximately every five years and the majority party is invited by the president of India to form a national government and elect a Prime Minister.

Elections in India, both Federal and State are very colourful and frantic affairs with posters and party flags hung everywhere from the largest cities to the smallest villages. For the fortunate visitor at the time of an election, all of India seems to take on an atmosphere of passionate festival as Indians from all walks of life and religions enjoy the process of deciding who will govern them and how.

EDUCATION

While in theory, all Indian children have the right to free elementary education, in practice, the nation is still struggling to keep its children in school in a basically agrarian society of small holdings where the demands of manual labour still draw heavily on youth.

Yet primary schools can be found in even the smallest villages throughout India where dedicated teachers make do with facilities that would be considered totally inadequate by western standards. Most larger towns have secondary education and the great cities of India boast universities with very high standards that have enabled their graduates to find professional employment not only in India but in many other highly developed western countries.

Increasing the literacy rate remains a constant target of the government - for public education on stemming the birth rate in a country of 800 million to be effective. While religious traditions, the desire for male progeny and a widely-held belief that many children will bring security to aged parents contribute to the population control problem, it is also apparent that increased literacy/education in adults can have an effect on the attitude of populate or perish.

COMMERCE AND INDUSTRY

With the departure of the British Raj, the leaders of newly- independent India had a grand design for the rapid industrialization of their country which, similarly to the People's Republic of China, was seen to depend on heavy industry and engineering. But, more than 40 years after independence, more than two thirds of the working population are still engaged in agriculture with much of this being inefficiently performed on small farms.

India's exports are still based mainly on textiles, Bombay having the largest textile industry. Specialized produce such as tea is an export money-earner but India has not been as successful as many third-world nations in creating successful light industry exports. Greater emphasis is now being placed on developing hi-tech industry with computers and other electronic goods in the forefront but India is still paying the price of protecting post-independence industries from foreign exports which resulted in minimizing the country's relatively cheap labour opportunities to develop industrially-based exports to the same extent as other Asian nations such as Taiwan, South Korea, Malaysia and Singapore.

There are some exceptions to this rule which has seen the possibility of a large automotive industry inhibited by protectionist policies. For instance, the Indian film making industry based in Bombay is the world's largest. Food production in India has been steadily increasing and, in the last two decades of the 20th century, the nation has achieved a food surplus and is steadily improving agricultural methods and the use of modern fertilizers should see India emerge as a significant exporter of agricultural products in the future.

India's main stock exchange is in Delhi. Most major industry is centred on the cities of Bombay and Calcutta with most heavy industry in or around the latter city.

RELIGIONS

Because India practises more religions than any other nation on earth, this section is longer than you will read in most of our other travel guides. The majority of Indians are adherents to the Hindu faith, almost 85 per cent. The second largest group is Muslim. In decreasing order come Christians, Sikhs, Buddhists and Jains. Judaism and Zoroastrianism (one of the world's oldest religions and practised by the Parsis of which Bombay has most), are also represented.

The oldest religion of all is Animism which is still professed by small groups of primitive tribespeople scattered in the southern mountain regions of the sub-continent.

Hinduism

Hinduism, which probably sprang from primitive Animism, has often been described by philosophers as more than a mere religion because of the unique lifestyle of its followers, coupled with an outlook of free thinking that does not prevent even an atheist from being a Hindu. In this sense, Hinduism is a way of life. The religion is not based on any single book of prophesy nor the revelation of any single teacher but on what Hindus see as Eternal Truth.

Unlike other great religions, Hinduism has few do and don't dogmas. It allows Hindus the freedom of their own individual search for spiritual experience and is extremely tolerant of all other faiths in the belief that the goal is the same. Hinduism recognises one god which, in the highest

form, is **Brahma**, the universal soul or spirit transcending time and space but who has physical representations in the form of Brahma, the creator, **Vishnu**, the preserver and **Shiva**, the destroyer and, paradoxically, also the rejuvenator.

There is a female counterpart to each of this trinity. Brahma's consort is **Saraswati** while Vishnu's companion is **Lakshmi** and Shiva's 'other half' is **Shakti**, worshipped as the mother of the world and symbolizing the power by which the one god creates then destroys the world only to recreate it again. One of the interesting facets of Hinduism that it absorbed many of the gods and rituals of successive conquerors of India from primitive times. These gods were all accepted by Hinduism in the belief that they represented the one great god whom other peoples knew by different names. The result in modern day Hinduism is a profusion of minor gods and goddesses.

A basic tenent of the religion, which has been absorbed by other religions in turn, is the belief in reincarnation. Hindus believe that their soul continues through cycles of birth, death and rebirth until that soul becomes one with Brahma, never to be reborn again. The law of **Karma** or 'action' is also a corner-stone of Hinduism. Basically, Karma embodies the law of cause and effect and is not unlike the Judaic belief that, as one sows, so one shall reap. A Hindu's thoughts, deeds and words in this life will determine the nature of reincarnation.

Hinduism also offers its devotees three paths to attain union with Brahma. Most Hindus choose the simplest through devotion and worship of a form of god, observing strictly their prayers, rituals and festivals. A second way to reach the one god is through action in the form of **Karma Yoga** where both men and women seek their goal through selfless service in their daily work. The final and most difficult pathway chosen by very few is that of **Jnana Yoga**, the way of knowledge and wisdom.

The Hindu scriptures direct that rituals and pilgrimmages to holy places are the first step in the pathway to the one god. A second way is in the worship of the one god through statues and images and the highest form is through mental worship and meditation.

The mystical syllable 'Om' is the symbol of Brahma.

Buddhism

Although this religion was born in India, it rapidly spread to neighbouring Asian countries, particularly China, so that now every fourth human being is a follower of Buddha. The religion's founder was born a prince in the 6th century BC. Prince **Siddhartha** was deeply moved by sickness, poverty and death that he saw beyond his palace walls and, at the age of 29, he left his royal life to seek the knowledge of teachers before embarking on a life of asceticism.

After nearly six years of meditation, he reached a state of enlightenment and commenced 45 years of preaching. He became **Gautama** or the **Buddha** and he taught his followers four truths to end human suffering. Buddha's followers also believe in the law of Karma and reincarnation although the Buddha himself never taught the concept of a one god or the individual soul. Some of the Buddha's teachings have been absorbed into Hinduism and Buddha became one of the Hindu pantheon as the ninth incarnation of Vishnu, the preserver.

Buddhists must not injure any living thing. They must not steal, live in an unchaste manner, lie, steal nor consume alcohol or drugs. While there are relatively few Buddhists in India today, the religion was spread by monks throughout central Asia, China and Japan, beginning under the rule of the great emperor Ashoka in the third century BC.

Jainism

Like Buddhism, Jainism arose as a reaction to the personal excesses of early Hindu priests but it has never created a following of any significance outside of India. Like Buddha, the founder of Jainism, **Vardhamana Mahavira** was born in the 6th century BC and renounced life as the son of a tribal chief to spend the next 12 years in a life of penance before reaching a state of the highest knowledge. He spent his remaining 30 years in spreading his doctrine of rejecting material possessions and not injuring any other creature.

Like Buddhism, Jainism does not embrace a creative god. But it holds the concept of a personal soul going through cycles of death and reincarnation to break the earthly bonds of Karma. Jainism has a strong following in India today and its adherents base their lives on simplicity of living, charity, humility and forgiveness of others.

Sikhism

The most recent of all of India's great religions, Sikhism emerged in the 15th century AD through its founder, the **Guru Nanak**, during a time of invasions and suffering in the **Punjab** region. Nanak's teachings were greatly influenced by **Kabir**, a saint recognised by both Hindus and Muslims. The essence of the Sikh religion as revealed by the Guru Nanak is the fatherhood of one god and the brotherhood of man. Sikhism also recognises that all religions are seeking to teach the same truths.

Because of this, devotees of all religions can follow the Sikh way of service to both man and god. The Sikh religion emphasizes the work ethic, family life, communal obligations and moral values. Personal prayer and meditation is the way by which the Sikh reaches towards god. While Sikhs also believe in reincarnation, the religion is essentially a bridge between Hinduism and Islam.

Zoroastrianism

Originally the main religion of Persia, Zoroastrianism was brought to India in the 7th century AD when many of its followers fled as Arab conquerors converted their country to Islam. In India, they became known as **Parsis**, a name stemming from the region of Pars in Persia from which the majority of religious refugees came. Today, India has the largest number of Zoroastrianists in the world.

The religion was founded by **Zarathusthra** who was also called **Zoroaster** and it recognizes one supreme god, **Ahura Mazda**, the wise creator. The Supreme Lord has the sun as his emblem while on earth he is symbolized by fire - which is why a fire is kept constantly burning in all Parsi temples.

Zoroaster taught of a constant conflict between good and evil spirits in the world with man having to choose a path between goodness and evil. The religion directs its

Republic Day Celebrations

India and Her People

followers towards a life of hard work, communal service and charity and it is very tolerant towards all other faiths. Because of this, a present day Parsi is free to visit the temples and churches of all other religions and, in India, they often do.

Because the Parsis worship the sanctity and purity of the elements fire, water, earth and air, they will neither bury nor cremate their dead. The body of a Parsi is left in a Tower of Silence where the corps is soon consumed by vultures.

Judaism

The coming of Jews to India traditionally dates from the first destruction of the Temple in Jerusalem in the 6th century BC. These Jews who had fled Palestine were believed to have been ship-wrecked close to present day Bombay and their descendents are known in India as **Black Jews**.

The second wave of Jews reached India in the first century BC following the destruction of the second Temple in Jerusalem by the Romans. Both groups fled to Cochin after persecution by Arabs in the 16th century. A third wave arrived in the 19th century and these settled in the main cities. Today there are only about 5,000 followers of Judaism in India and, in recent years, many of India's Jews have migrated to Israel and western countries. Those remaining enjoy a life free of any form of anti semitism.

India and Her People

Christianity

Christ's apostle, **St. Thomas** was believed to have come to India in about 54 AD before Christianity reached Europe. The early Syrian Christians built a Church to St. Thomas in Kerala on the Malabar Coast close to the present-day city of Trivandram. St. Thomas is said to have crossed southern India and settled in a village near the modern city of Madras where he spent many years seeking to teach the words of Jesus Christ before being killed by a group who resented his evangelism.

Today's visitors to Madras can see a small cave on a low hill close to the Madras airport in which, tradition holds, the early Christian martyr lived. There is a second legend in India that points to **St Bartholemew** being the first Christian missionary to visit and, even before the Renaissance, historians of the Middle Ages made references to Christian settlements in India. Legend and tradition changed to history with the arrival of **St. Francis Xavier** in western India in 1542 following the Portugese conquest of Goa. St Francis Xavier, whose casket is in the Church of the Born Jesus in Old Goa, draws Catholic pilgrims in their thousands to Goa each year.

The saint was followed by a wave of Portugese missionaries who travelled widely in India, some of them reaching the court of the Moghul emperor **Akbar** the Great

India and Her People

Carrion Birds near Taj Mahal

and unsuccessfully attempting to convert him to Christianity.

After the Portugese, Catholic missionaries from other parts of Europe entered India and these were followed in the 18th century by protestant missionaries, particularly from Germany, Denmark and Holland. But the key to the spread of modern Christianity was the arrival of the British and their conquest of India resulted in an ascendency of the Anglican denomination above those which had come before.

Through two centuries of the British Raj, foreign missionaries spread throughout India and were particularly active in the more primitive tribal regions. India's Christians have contributed vastly to social welfare and education as well as providing medical and nursing support to the poor. The contribution of the Christian faith to modern Indian society is far greater than could be expected from the relatively small proportion of India's 800 million people who follow the way of Jesus Christ.

This evangelical zeal and selfless humanitarianism was exemplified by such people as Mother Teresa. The father of independent India, Mahatma Gandhi, although not a Christian, was deeply influenced by its teachings and many of his most famous speeches and writings are punctuated with quotations from the New Testament.

India and Her People

Islam

Arab traders were the first to bring the teachings of the prophet **Mohammed** to India in the 7th century and they were followed by successive invasions by Muslims until the beginning of the 13th century. This saw the establishment of the first Muslim overlordship in Delhi. Muslim power extended from this base until only the most southern part of India was independent of Muslim India.

The great Moghul Empire was created in 1506 by **Barbur**. The greatest of his successors was **Akbar** who ruled from 1556 to 1605 and whose policy of religious tolerance brought a more-or-less lasting peace between Hindus and Muslims. Akbar's vision was continued by two others - Kabir and Nanak and Nanak the Guru who founded the Sikh religion with the goal of increasing mutual tolerance between Hindus and Muslims.

Islam's spirit of brotherhood has played a part in loosening the Indian caste system. The teachings of the prophet embodied in the Holy Koran are not far removed from those of the Old Testament of the Christian Bible. Islam recognizes only one god - Allah. The relative simplicity of Islam was a force in influencing Hindus to question the value of many of their traditional rituals yet, in India, the interaction of these two great faiths has resulted in aesthetic expression through poetry, music, art and architecture.

Dancing Monkey

India and Her People

THE PEOPLES OF INDIA

Modern ethnologists agree that in the mists of pre-history, the Indian sub-continent was sparsely populated by a race of Negroid people possessing a primitive culture and probably related to aboriginal tribes still to be found in parts of Sri Lanka and the Indonesian island of Sumatra. It is still debated whether this race was ethnically linked with the Australoid tribes of Australia.

While still in an era of pre-history, India was invaded by other races from western Asia that have loosely been called **Dravidians**. These people slowly penetrated to the far south to be followed by a smaller infiltration of Mongol races from central Asia which entered the country from the north east. The blending of these two invading peoples with the original Aborigines is thought to have been completed when wave after wave of Aryan people swept into India through the mountain passes in the north-west.

The Aryan invaders in turn were mostly absorbed and this has resulted in seven distinct racial types to be found in modern India. Examples of the original Aboriginal race can still be identified with primitive tribal people of the jungles and mountains of southern and central India.

The Dravidian race can be distinctly identified throughout the south as far north as the Valley of the Ganges. A blending of Indo-Aryan races is more or less distinct to the regions of Rajasthan and the Punjab. The great majority of modern Hindus are a mixture of Aryan and Dravidian stock emanating from the Gangetic Valley but extending westward with a further blending of Indo-Aryan people has occurred.

Another distinct sub-race is the **Scytho-Dravidian** type found east of the Indus River. In Assam and the foothills of the eastern Himalayas, the people are of distinct **Mongul** inheritance, quite clearly related to the present population of China and Tibet. India's seventh distinct racial type are **Mongolo-Dravidians** who also appear to possess elements of Indo-Aryan blood and these people are represented principally in west Bengal.

The English, of course, made their impact too, along with the Portugese to an earlier, lesser extent. There are pockets of Anglo-Indians in various parts, notably Goa where the visitor will also meet Indians who could have been born in modern Lisbon.

It is hard to recognize all origins when you are visiting on a holiday. But the Sikh men are discernable for their colourful turbans beneath which all hair, never cut, is neatly wound. The dab of cosmetic colour worn by many Indian women on the forehead above the nose (and sometimes be-jewelled) is to aid beauty. They contrast with Muslim women who, if deeply religious, conceal their faces.

The traveller is more likely to pick by dress the religion of an Indian rather than his/her ethnic background. Then again, that dress may reflect the region from which the individual comes, for example the Punjab or Kashmir.

MEETING PEOPLE

Amongst a population of 800 million, you can't help but meet the people and sometimes you would prefer not to be confronted with the many willing and often too insistent residents pressing you to hire, buy or give. If you don't want to do any of these, be very firm in your refusal.

In a country where much poverty abounds, it is natural for travellers to feel threatened or at risk. India is not an easy country to explore because of it. But on the road or rails, in the air and in your accommodations you will find many Indians who are as eager to share conversations and experiences with a foreigner as you are to discover friendly people with similar aims.

Indians generally are gregarious and warmly eager to impart their knowledge of their history, culture and lifestyles. They are delighted to be greeted in the traditional manner of forming the hands in front of the chest into a near pyramid, as Christians join their hands when saying 'Amen.' This should be accompanied by the Hindi word '**Namaste**,' meaning good morning/afternoon/evening or night. If you are greeted with Namaskaar and the same gesture, you will have been told: 'My guest is as my god.'

Perhaps the best way in which to make friends is to wait a few moments when encountering a stranger. If he/she makes no hire/buy/give approaches, it is then up to you to open the conversation. This inevitably produces a friendly response. Indian travellers are invariably polite and helpful as are hotel staffs and tourism officers. While a man will appreciate a westerner's handshake, an Indian woman may feel a touch unwelcome. Some may not respond to being addressed by a man, foreigner or local, which is the right of woman of the world - any part. But female foreigner can politely speak to Indian male and, provided she is not provocative in her manner or dress, can expect to be treated with respect. If she is too bare of arm, leg or breast, she can expect to face the consequences she would experience in any other country.

At times of festival, Hindu in particular, some Indians may spontaneously invite visitors to share their joy of the occasion, even invoking strangers off the street to join

India and Her People

them under a marquee for a celebration, such as **Dussehra**, particularly in Delhi (see festivals.) Do not refuse these marvellous opportunities to meet the Indian people at their most exciting and excitable.

Home stays can be arranged in some Indian cities, giving visitors opportunity to interact with families and understand the Indian way of life. Also some cities, Bombay included, have programmes in which the traveller can meet Indian families in their homes. Contact the Government of India Tourist Office.

Gandhi's Tomb

INFOTIP: Do not be offended if you invite an Indian to join you for a drink that he/she refuses alcohol. It may be against their religion so do offer an alternative.

India and Her People

Birla Temple

INDIAN LANGUAGES

Just as India's population represents a diversity and blending of races, the many languages and dialects used across the great sub-continent are varied. For most visitors using this Info- India, English will be understood by the majority of people they will encounter in the major cities and larger towns. But being able to use even a few words and phrases of the official Indian language - **Hindi** - is a sure way of expressing true interest and friendship with the Indian people and it can be fun as well. In Delhi, Urdu is also widely spoken.

There are many English words used in modern Hindi but in the Roman alphabet their spellings reflect pronunciation with an Indian accent. Example: The English word 'station' would be pronounced as 'steshan' in Hindi. As a guide to

India and Her People

approximately correct pronunciation of Hindi words and phrases that follow, the visitor needs to understand Hindi pronunciation of vowels, consonants and diphthons.

a	as in focal
ar	as in father
au	as in laundry
ai	as in wait
e	as in they
i	as in din
ee	as in feet
o	as in old
u	as in put
oo	as in soon
ch	as in teach
d	as in drama
gh	as in ghost
j	as in jet
kh	as in loch
n	as in French (pronounced nasally)
ph	as in physical
r	as in drive
th	as in think
y	as in yellow

If the traveller in India leaves the major tourist routes and has trouble being understood by non-English speakers, it is advisable to ask for the police station as officers in even the smallest centres will have an understanding of English. The Hindi words for police station are **tharnar pulis chowki**. The next most important phrase for visitors to any country is 'Where is a toilet?' With a little bit of luck, you will solve the problem by saying '**Gusalkhana kakan hai?**'

A few other useful words and phrases in Hindi are:

man	ardmee
woman	aurat
yes, please	ji, harn
Good morning/afternoon/night	Namaste
Please call a taxi	Kripaya ek taxee bularo
slowly	dheere
stop	ruko
Call a porter please	Portar ko bularo
Show me the menu	Mujhe meenoo kard dikharo
Clean the room	Kamrar sarf karo
The bill, please	Bill laro
May I know your name?	Arpkar shubh narm?

India and Her People

Where is the tourist office?	Toorist arfis kaharn hai?
I want a guide	Mujhe ek garid charhiye
Thank you	Shukriyar
What is the price of this?	Iskee-kyar keemat hai?
Post this letter	Yeh khat leter-baks men darlo
Where is the post and telegraph office?	Dark aur tar ghar kaharn hai?
What is your telephone number?	Apkar telefon nambar?
I am sorry	Mujhe afsos hai
Don't touch this	Ise mat chhuo
Bring the doctor	Daktar ko bularo
What is the time?	Kyar bajar hai?
Where is the bank?	Bank kaharn hai?

Numbers

one	ek	six	chhe
two	do	seven	sart
three	teen	eight	arth
four	char	nine	nau
five	parnch	ten	das
20	bees	80	assee
30	tees	90	nabbe
40	charlees	100	sau
50	pachars	1000	hazar
60	sarth	100,000	larkh
70	sattar		

HISTORY AND CULTURE

The history of civilization in India spans nearly 5,000 years and only China can similarly boast of an unbroken line in cultural development through such a long period. As with Egypt and Mesapotamia, the annual inundations of India's great rivers produced a richness of soil and an ease of agriculture resulting in a food surplus which is essential to the emergence of an urban-style civilization.

India's earliest urban development dates from about 2,500 BC and, since its discovery in the 1920s, is referred to by archaeologists as the Indus Valley Civilization. Although the two largest cities of Mohenjodaro and Harappa are now in Pakistan, smaller sites have been excavated in the Punjab and the States of Gujarat and

India and Her People

> **INFOTIP:** While cutlery will be supplied to visitors, it is acceptable to eat, particularly frontier food, with your right hand which adds another sensory perception to your enjoyment. Don't allow the food to rise up into your palm but use fingers. It's easy to become adept.

Victory Tower

Rajasthan, indicating that the civilization was widespread through north west India and what today is eastern Pakistan.

The major excavations have revealed the remains of sophisticated cities and towns laid out on a grid pattern of intersecting streets with clearly defined socio-economic localities as well as public buildings and communal graneries. The **Indus Valley** culture produced artifacts in copper, bronze, lead and tin and bricks were fired in kilns. These early Indian city dwellers had also developed a pictographic form of writing which so far has defied experts' attempts to translate.

Evidence has emerged that the culture had regular

trading relations with the tribal areas of India adjacent to it as well as with other early civilizations such as Sumer in Iraq. These people appear to have had a formalized religion, worshipping both male and female gods. Consistent flooding of the settlements along the Indus river and adjacent to it is believed to have gradually led to a decline in this culture which seemed to have practically disappeared by the time of the first great *Aryan* invasions of India around 1,500 BC.

The *Aryans* were a people originated in central Asia and their hymns, known as the **Vedas**, have been the cornerstone of the Hindu religion. The ancient **Hindus** were a remarkable people who, among other things, are attributed with conceiving the decimal system and algebra. The Aryans were originally cattle-herding, tribal nomads but, in India, they rapidly turned to agriculture, no doubt learned from the remaining people they had conquered, most of whom, it seems, were turned into slaves.

The Indian system of caste can be traced to the Aryan invasions and caste was formally known as varna -literally colour - as a distinction between the fair-skinned Aryans and their darker- complexioned slaves. From this simple division developed class distinctions between the Aryans themselves, resulting in the caste of priests (*Brahmana,*)

Outside Qutab Minar Complex

India and Her People

warriors (*Kshatiya*,) artisans and merchants (*Vaishya*) and farmers (*Shudra*.) Later with the refinement of Hinduism came the non-caste of the Untouchable, the lowest of menial workers so reviled that if his shadow touched that of someone of higher status, the latter would have to be cleansed of the contact by ritual.

The Aryan tribes worshipped gods related to the natural elements of sun, water, fire and wind. A milestone in India's civilization occurred in about 1,000 BC with the discovery of iron and the efficiency of the iron axe in creating arable land from forest areas resulted in a rapid growth of population, production and trade.

Another natural result of this development was a constant warring between small communities, resolved as in China, with the emergence of the first empire on the sub-continent. The most famous figure in this **Maurya Empire** was **Ashoka** who ruled from 269 BC to 232 BC. Even before the rise of the **Maurya Dynasty**, India had become aware of the Greek civilization far to the west through the invasion of north-west India by *Alexander the Great* in 327 BC. Alexander and his armies left a legacy of Macedonian culture and even today the sculpture and art of the areas of the Punjab that he reached have a defineable Greek influence.

The Mauryan empire fell apart soon after the death of

Ashoka and India was once again invaded by several peoples out of Asia. At about this time, India's second great empire emerged. Although not as great as the one that had preceded it, the **Gupta dynasty** held sway approximately 200 years and the rulers of this dynasty commenced significant trade with the Greek and Roman civilizations of Europe while a spirit of learning and sophisticated culture spread throughout the empire.

During the same period, the **Chola kingdom** had emerged in what is now the **Tamil Nadu** region of south west India. The Gupta age also saw a flourishing of Hinduism, literature, astronomy, mathematics and drama. But the empire gradually declined and, with it, India's trading links. This led to a greater dependence on rural economy.

Although the soils of India were rich, water had been a constant problem and it was not until the 8th century AD that the development of irrigation, utilizing a geared wheel drawn by oxen, resulted in significant expansion of agricultural production.

The 8th century also saw the beginning of Muslim invasions through the north-west passes of India and these incursions - originally more-or-less raids - resulted, over 400 years, in the establishment of Muslim-dominated territories in northern India. The best known of these areas was the **Delhi Sultanate**, the boundaries of which fluctuated quite dramatically the three centuries of its existence.

As the sultanate weakened, northern India represented a glittering prize to any central Asian chieftain with a strong army behind him and the most devastating raid was carried out by **Timur** in 1398. Some 130 years after Timur laid waste to the remaining territories of the Delhi Sultanate, India was again invaded by one of his descendents - the founder of the great **Mughal empire, Zahiruddin Mohammad Babur**. Babur's grandson was **Akbar** who extended the **Mughal rule** throughout northern India and a large part of southern India between 1556 and 1605.

Although only a teenager when he ascended the throne, Akbar swiftly improved the bureaucratic and military systems inherited from the days of the Delhi Sultanate and, although illiterate, he patronized religion, art and science. Akbar's reign also saw a blending of both Islamic and Hindu styles of architecture.

The emperor's successors never achieved Akbar's grandeur and when, in the 17th century, India witnessed the arrival of the trading adventurers from the major maritime nations of western Europe, the sub-continent was in a state of potential weakness - the traditional open invitation to any conqueror. The first among these

India and Her People

newcomers - the Portugese - were quickly followed by Dutch, French and English and the early individual contacts were soon replaced by formalized companies trading in silk, cotton and spices.

By 1707, the great *Mughal empire* had begun to disintegrate into smaller regional sultanates and kingdoms and both the English and French East India companies were alert to exploit this situation while, in turn, fighting among themselves for trade supremacy.

The Europeans were not the only ones to exploit the fragmentation of the empire and, in 1739, the Persian ruler **Nadir Shar** attacked and plundered Delhi, departing with, among other loot, the world famous *Peacock throne* and the *Koh-i-Noor diamond*.

Mahatma Gandhi's Grave

Although the Portugese remained in Goa until after the emergence of modern independent India, the Dutch East India Company withdrew from its early Indian concessions to concentrate on what is today Indonesia. After several decades of intrigue and minor battles, the British outwitted the French interests to emerge as the major western colonizing power.

India and Her People

British power stemmed from the defeat of the ruler of Benghal first in 1757 and again in 1765. By the end of the 18th century, the British East India Company was actively and successfully planning the extension of its rule originally based in the small trading concessions at Madras and Calcutta.

During the first decades of the 19th century, the institution, to be known as the **Raj**, emerged as the British extended their hold and influence over a large part of the sub- continent. By 1857, what had been known as the British empire in India had become known as the British Empire of India.

Statue of Gandhi

India and Her People

The exploitation of the British led to ever-mounting resentment among most stratas of Indian society, from the weakened rulers through intellectuals and artisans to the impoverished peasantry. The fuse to this potential powder keg was lit in 1857 by a seemingly minor incident which still epitomized the English indifference to Indian religious and cultural traditions.

The British East India Company had acquired a new type of musket cartridge in which their native troops or sepoys were required to bite a hole before inserting it into the weapon. A rumour was spread that these cartridges were greased with the fat from both cows and pigs. This offended both Muslim and Hindu troops as the Hindus held the cow as sacred and eating of beef as sinful while the Muslims were forbidden by their religion to touch pork which was considered unclean.

The sepoys at *Meerut* near Delhi rebelled, sparking what has become known as the great Indian mutiny. The Indian troops marched on Delhi where they were joined by other sepoys who had killed their British officers. From Delhi, the revolt rapidly spread throughout northern and central India, engulfing not only soldiers but civiians in towns and villages. The Indians had placed the previously powerless *Mughal emperor* at their head and the resulting fight to the finish was eventually won by the English through superior arms and military tactics and their control over railways and telegraph lines.

Although the mutiny lasted 18 months and produced many Indian heroes and heroines, it culminated in the strengthening of English supremacy in India and a policy of dividing Hindu from Muslim by discriminating against Muslims in many areas of employment. The mutiny also sounded the death-knell of British East India Company power and in 1858, by an act of the British parliament, the administration of all territory in India passed to the British Crown.

The mutiny also brought about a fast expansion of the British army in India with far greater emphasis being placed on British rather than native Indian troops and the use of this army to suppress any form of protest against British rule or that of Indian princes whom the English still recognized.

But the dream of a re-emergence of Indian independence was not dead and in 1915, the long road towards it was begun with the return to India from South Africa of one of the 20th century's most remarkable men, **Mohandas Karamchand Gandhi**. Otherwise known as **Mahatma Gandhi**, he, in South Africa, had experienced bitter humiliation over the colour of his skin. He commenced to organize Indian victims of white-British tyranny into a non-violent protest movement. Before Gandhi's real campaign commenced, he embarked on personal journeys throughout most of India's regions, familiarizing himself with the poverty and suffering of the ordinary people.

In 1920, he launched a vast non-cooperation movement which, within two years, saw mass participation throughout India. Both Hindus and Muslims buried their differences in a united struggle against their British masters. By the end of the 1920s, Gandhi had found allies among other Indian nationalists such as **Jawaharlal Nehru** and **Subhash Chandra Bose** and their Indian *Congress Party*.

In 1930, a second wave of civil disobedience began. It was dramatized by Gandhi through one of the most elementary of human needs - salt. The British government had monopolized the manufacture of salt and the revenue received from it and Gandhi set out with his followers on a 250 km walk to the sea on the **Gujarat Coast**, declaring that he would make his own salt and pay no tax. Gandhi was joined along the route by scores of thousands of his fellow Indians, both men and women, from all sections of Indian society. The British met this confrontation quite violently but the atrocities resulted in popular revulsion among the people in Britain and the government called a round- table conference in London where the representatives of several Indian poltical groups were invited to confer on the future of India.

The time was not yet ripe for the British to even contemplate the demands of the Congress Party for Indian independence and, after these London negotiations collapsed, the civil disobedience movement in India began again, defying every form of repression unleashed by the British government.

The progression of the Indian struggle for independence was virtually halted by world war two in Europe then, despite being one of the victorious allies, the end of six years of conflict saw Great Britain without the military and economic power to continue to suppress the Indian demand for freedom.

Early in 1947, the British government acknowledged the inevitable and the decision to withdraw from India was made. But Britain had made its decision conditional on the partition of the sub-continent to create a new **State of Pakistan**. This was to occupy two regions - one in the west and the other nearly 2,000 km away in Indian territory in what had been **British East Bengal**. The birth of independent India on August 15, 1947 had already been heralded by a tremendous upheaval of religious violence and bloodshed as Hindus within the area to become

India and Her People

Pandit Nehru's Grave

Pakistan and Muslims within India proper sought to migrate between the two new nations.

It was a bitter experience for the peace-loving Gandhi who, in a small house in Calcutta, wept at the outburst of destruction and death. This, perhaps noblest of all of 20th century humanitarians, was assassinated in January 1948.

Independent India's first Prime Minister was *Jawaharlal Nehru*. He instituted a policy of maintaining not only neutrality for the newly-independent nation but good relationships with Great Britain - which did not endear him to many of his fellow Indians.

Despite Nehru's avowed adherence to Gandhi's philosophy of peaceful confrontation, India was involved in three military confrontations with neighbouring Pakistan in the first 24 years of its independence. Besides these conflicts, triggered by border disputes involving Kashmir and Bangladesh, these first two decades of independence also witnessed military incidents with China. The policy of non-alignment pushed India towards the Soviet Union through American support for Pakistan. Nehru, more commonly known as **Pandit Nehru**, was followed by **Indira Gandhi** until her assassination in 1984 by disgruntled Sikh extremists who were members of her personal body-guard. Her son **Rajiv Gandhi** became Prime Minister following her death.

India and Her People

The first 40 or so years of Indian independence has seen the encouragement of foreign investment and increasing industrialization backed during the 1980s with an emphasis on imported technology by the United States, Europe and Japan. The middle class of India has begun to flourish but the nation has not shed inherent difficulties of race and religion epitomized by the struggles of the *Sikhs* in the *Punjab* for an independent identity and the Indian support for the *Tamil* population in neighbouring Sri Lanka.

While supposedly no longer recognized, India's age-old caste system is still an inhibiting factor to efficient national development and women still struggle for their own independence in a society in which some sections continue to believe in arranged marriages, the dowry system, bride burning and the inevitability of a widow dying on her husband's funeral pyre.

For a vast nation which, in the second half of the 20th century, has emerged as the world's most populous western style democracy, India's greatest achievement must be its success in feeding its people while avoiding centralized dictatorships of either the left or the right. Neither the Soviet Union nor the People's Republic of China have succeeded in this common goal.

Slowly but surely, India's policy of industrial modernization has placed it in 10th position of the industrialized nations of the world.

Jama Masjid, the Great Mosque

INDIA'S GLORIOUS ARCHITECTURE

One only has to drive through the villages and observe the manner in which the Indian women style cow pats into neat, visually attractive structures drying for future use as fuel or fertilizer, to realize how inherent is the artistry of construction within the souls of the people. The cow pats and also the haystacks of varied sizes and shapes that draw the visitor from a vehicle to photograph against a backdrop of clear sky and scenic interest, are works of art.

India's architecture, as impermanent as a haystack and a shrine-like stack of cow pats, or as enduring as the *Taj Mahal*, is as much a reflection of its people's creativity as its history and religions. The visitor to India will inevitably be exposed to the architecture of at least two millenia and an understanding of the development of India's unique buildings is essential to its appreciation. The traditions stretch back to the mists of pre-history and the great **Indus Valley Civilization** where both sun-dried and fired bricks were used to create quite sophisticated private and communal structures in the large cities of *Harappa, Mohenjodaro, Lothal* and *Kalibangan*.

The technique of the arch had been mastered by these ancient people and the excavation of the **Great Bath** at Mohenjodaro is proof that ritualistic public buildings had been created at that time. This first flowering of practical and decorative architecture was swept away into a dark age that followed the Aryan invasions and, for nearly 2,000 years, Indian building and architecture languished in simple structures of circular huts with domed roofs until the medium of stone suddenly appeared in the third and second centuries BC.

Stone buildings have been linked with the emergence of the Buddhist religion and many of the earliest examples have survived until the present day. The first use of stone centred around the building of the stupa or funerary mound and progressed to a hall of worship and then a monastery. The earliest examples show a reflection in stone of the wooden structures that preceded them. Early Buddhist architecture frequently was created around natural caves where large prayer halls were excavated and the monk/architects introduced stone carvings to pillars and rafters.

In the centuries that followed, a tremendous expansion and diversity occured in religious architecture, principally under the great *Gupta dynasty* and even recently-built Hindu temples still bear the influence of this period. During these centuries, the temple evolved from the simple square chamber that existed in early Gupta shrines in central India to quite elaborate structures and, in the later

India and Her People

Government Building at night

Gupta period, there emerged the temple spire that became the characteristic feature of Hindu temple architecture. It appeared in two forms. In the north, it was known as the *shikhara* and was smoothly pyramidal, rising to a rounded top with a pointed tip. In the south, the spire, known as the *vimana*, soared in a series of diminishing steps, similar to the stepped pyramids of early Egypt and Mexico.

The earliest of these spires were evident in the 6th century temples in what is now the **State of Karnataka** but their final peak of refinement came at **Mahabalipuram** near **Madras** in the 8th century where they were fashioned from outcrops of rock. The temple architecture was further refined between the 10th and 13th centuries and the finest examples of this era are found at **Khajuraho** in central India, where the sculptures to be seen today are incredibly erotic, **Thanjavur** in the south and at **Konarak** in the east. Intricate carvings covering these remarkable buildings were reflections of the life of the people. At **Tamil Nadu**, vestibules called gudha mandapas and towering gateways known as gopurams became part of temple design.

During the Hoysala dynasty from the 11th to the 14th century, the northern and southern styles blended and the form of the shikhara and the vimana were amalgamated

India and Her People

into a bell-shaped tower above a star-shaped shrine. The temple facades were richly decorated with sculptures of gods and their consorts.

Early Muslim invaders of India had no influence on traditional Hindu architecture but, after the 13th century and the first Muslim conquest, a new tradition of building began to emerge. An early Muslim king, **Qutb-ud-din Aibak** who became ruler of Delhi, commanded to be built the first mosque in India. His architects wrecked existing Hindu and Jain temples for the raw material of this mosque which was a hotch potch of design and building expediency between the Muslim overseers and their subjugated Hindu stone masons.

The subsequent history of Muslim architecture in India is a story of gradual fusion of two opposite religious ideals into the richest period of design and construction. Most of the monumental buildings over the next 500 years were memorials to the vanity of rulers and, with the establishment of the **Mughal empire**, an era of unparalleled building activity commenced. Architects and artisans from every part of India were given free reign to express their ideas in stone and the resulting mixture of both Hindu and Muslim styles were many and varied.

Most buildings during Akbar's long reign were constructed of sandstone but his son **Jahangir** preferred

India and Her People

the lustre of pure white marble although he was not an outstanding builder and liked to express his creativity in the laying out of Moghul gardens. Jahangir's successor, **Shahjahan** renewed the Moghul building frenzy and took the traditions of Moghul architecture to their climactic best in the famous **Taj Mahal at Agra**.

Shahjahan was responsible for the city of **Shahjahanabad** at Delhi and, in the seraglio (harem building,) there is a profusion of luxuriously embellished marble pavilions surrounded by gardens and water channels. Shahjahan's son, **Aurangzeb** ruled the slowly disintegrating Moghul empire for 60 years during which period no great work of architecture was created.

The coming of the British to India put an effective end to indigenous Indian architecture with the invaders' determination to erect uncompromising copies of Greek, Renaissance and Gothic buildings created from plans and sketches imported from England. To a lesser extent, the Portugese, French and Dutch reflected the architecture of their homelands on the buildings they erected in India. While some of these monumental edifaces were almost

Delhi Vista

India and Her People

grudgingly embellished with motifs from the Indian traditions, the basic forms were definitely western.

When India achieved independence in 1947, Prime Minister Nehru called for the development of a truly Indian architecture but the first attempts by the new nation's designers were somewhat awkward imitations of the past. Nehru insisted on a new and vital style of contemporary architecture and commissioned the Frenchman, *Corbusier*, to build a capital city for the new State of the Punjab at *Chandigarh*.

Corbusier planned the city in a scheme of integrated sectors and introduced to visual expression the forms of raw concrete and his now-famous bries soleil or sun breakers which shaded windows from a number of angles. The renowned Frenchman set the pattern for what is now recognized as modern Indian architecture, laying great stress on functionalism and economy.

Currently architecture is in a state of flux throughout India. In many regions, architects are recognising the great importance of local conditions and are creating buildings that, while utilitarian, pose no threat to the aesthetics of their environment.

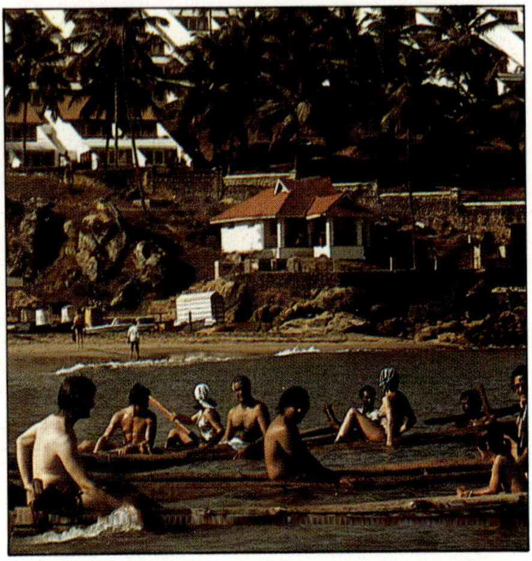

PART II
Sightseeing

Bilar Temple

DELHI

3000 YEARS OF HISTORY

Although many aspects of Delhi's three millenia of history have been touched upon earlier, the visitor is helped by an elementary understanding of the modern capital's continuous and colourful past, believed by archaeologists to have commenced in about 1000 BC as the legendary main city of the Aryan invaders, **Indraprastha**.

In recent years, extensive archaeological digs have brought to light evidence of this first settlement's flourishing existence. From about 300 BC to the present day, there have been seven significant cities in and around the current area of New Delhi.

The first was **Lal Kot**, dating from the middle of the 11th century and created by the **Tomar Dynasty** king, **Anangpal**. His capital was sacked by the **Chauhan Rajputs** less than a century later. The latter years of the 12th century saw the first consolidation of Islamic power, a result of which was the destruction of more than a score of **Hindu** and **Jain** temples to provide material for the first mosques at **Qutab Minar Complex**.

The second second city of Delhi was **Sira**, established just before the turn of the 13th century by the most famous of the **Khilji Dynasty** rulers, **Sultan Ala-ud-din**.

The next city to rise was **Tughlakabad**, the creation of **Ghias-ud-din** during his brief five year reign. The demise of this massive settlement has been attributed to an inadequate water supply and, today, there are only scattered ruins to remind the visitor of its passing glory.

Jahanpanah, built by **Mohammed Shah Tughlak**, the fourth city, rose to the north of *Siri*. It too was soon abandoned when this capricious king decided to move his capital and his subjects more than 1000 km south west to the **Deccan Plateau**. In less than 20 years, the move proved to be a disaster. Its survivors faced the long march back to Delhi where their descendents became citizens of **Ferozabad**, the fifth city commenced in 1351 by **Feroz Shah Tughlak**.

Today there is hardly a trace left of this city which fronted the **Jamuna river**. The city was torn apart in the 17th century by **Shah Jahan** who used its bricks and stone to build his own capital of **Shahjahanabad**.

Virtually nothing now remains of a sixth city built by the Afghan **Emperor Sher Shah** except a few tombs and mosques in the area known today as the **Lodi Gardens**.

Delhi

From the start of the 16th century, the court was moved to **Agra** and there followed a long period of alternating between Delhi and Agra before the seventh city of **Shahjahanabad**, which still exists as Old Delhi, was created in the two centuries following its foundation in 1638.

The 18th century saw the rise of British power throughout India and, in 1911, *King George V* announced the transfer of the Raj's capital from Calcutta to Delhi which resulted in the creation of New Delhi.

GRACE OF EMPIRES

'Here we stand in Delhi, symbol of old and new. We feel the good and the bad of India in Delhi city which has been the grace of many empires and the nursery of a republic.'
Jawaharlal Nehru

Think of Washington DC and Rome, the open landscaped spaces surrounding important buildings in the former, the grand monuments of the latter. Add seven million people, the spectacle of festival, the atmosphere of a mingling of centuries and cultures, the excitement and intrigue of being an international political centre and you have the throbbing heart of the world's largest democracy and the tingling nervous system of a nation.

India's capital city, and its third largest metropolis, Delhi lives in both past and present, as ancient as its legendary history of being a city divided into seven townships and as modern as the skyscrapers towering over Old Delhi. The old city's labyrinth of unnamed lanes and ways around the *Red Fort* and the *New Delhi* of wide avenues, gardens, impressive buildings and mansions began to merge in 1913 after it became the capital under the British in 1911. Formerly, India's capital was Calcutta.

The recorded history of Delhi dates back to the 15th century when it was a flourishing city, the Muslim capital of India, having previously known Hindu rule. Then, successively came *Persians, Afghans, Turks, Moghals* and the *British* in the 1800s. They sought to glorify the grandeur of the British Empire in the creation of New Delhi. For centuries, Delhi's location has made it a city of tremendous strategic importance. But Delhi's history, ancient and more modern, is best traced as you discover its monuments and attractions.

Set in the north, almost in a direct line high longtitudinally from the central tip of the finger of southern India, Delhi is on the west bank of the **Yamuna River** and bordered by the **States of Haryana** and **Uttar Pradesh**. It derived its name either from **Raja Dillu**, the 8th century king of

Kannauj, or from the first of the seven medieaval townships, **Dhillika**. Then known as **Dehalli, Dilli** or **Dehiz**, it finally became Delhi.

The capital is the jumping off place for other intriguing parts of the north, *Agra, Jaipur, Varanasi* and *Srinagar*, above Delhi in fabled Kashmir.

Delhi encompasses about 1500 square kilometres of which around 600 square km are urban. The 17th century old walled city still has streets without names. While New Delhi is well laid out, almost on a spokewheel principal from central **Connaught Place**, it is not really a walking city because it is so spacious and its attractions, often set in large grounds, are more scattered the further from the hub of the wheel they extend.

> **INFOTIP:** Unless you are a footslogger or are wandering the central core, take a tourist taxi or, if you are brave, hop on a bus or train and let's go. Alternatives are tours.

OLD DELHI, DEFENCES AND DELIGHTS

The Red Fort (Lal Qila)

While not the most northerly of Delhi's monuments, nor its oldest, The Red Fort is one of India's most magnificent palaces and the place on the edge of Old Delhi which most visitors make priority in case time runs out to see everything the city offers.

To orientate yourself, it is down from the Interstate bus terminal on **Qudsia Road**, which is opposite the garden of the same name. (This includes a camping site.) The terminal is close to the easterly intersection with the long **Mahatma Gandhi Road** which runs parallel and south beside the river and behind the fort. Alternatively, you can proceed westwards from the terminal until you reach **Lothian Road**, and turn left and south to see on the way the **Kashmiri Gate** where bitter fighting took place when the English recaptured Delhi during the Mutiny.

So-named Red Fort after the sandstone used to built its 2.5 km surrounding walls, the fort has two main entrances, the **Delhi Gate** well down if you are arriving from the south along **Netaji Subhash Road** or the **Lahore Gate** which is similarly constructed. This gate faces **Chandni Chowk**, the city's most infamous thoroughfare.

After an 11-year reign at Agra, the powerful Moghul ruler **Shah Jehan** transferred his capital to Delhi and, after nine years, the fort was completed in 1648. Shah Jehan didn't

Delhi

see his rule out here however, having been imprisoned by his son **Aurangzeb** to die in the Agra Fort. Originally lavish with unbelievable riches, the towered fort has survived earthquake.

Through the *Lahore Gate*, one enters a vaulted hall, now comprising 36 shops on two floors, previously a courtiers' market place. Next is a grass-centred courtyard, the **Naubat Khana**, once a setting in which Moghul court bands used play all day. The **Diwan-i-Am** is a building with arcaded cloisters round the courtyard. Here, after processions of horses, decorated elephants, the army and presentations to the emperor, he would hear from his gem-encusted sanctuary applications for justice from his subjects.

'If there be paradise on the earth, it is this, it is this, it is this.'

In Persian letters, this inscription is above an arch in the central hall of **Diwan-i-Khas**. It is a marble pavilion formerly with jewelled hall and silver ceiling (looted of its Peacock throne, silver and jewelled panels respectively by Nadir Shah, the Marathas and British but partly restored by Lord Curzon.) This was a paradise of private audiences for the emperor and friends but also a hell for two of his brothers murdered by the unstable, insecure Aurangzeb.

North of the Diwan-i-Khas are three interconnecting marble apartments, collectively known as **Khas-Mahal**. They comprise a house of worship, bed chamber and conversation house.

Red Ford

Between the bedchamber and place of worship is the **Scale of Justice**, gold inlaid moon and stars on a carved marble screen, made to show the emperor's justice was weighed like a scale.

Near the Diwan-e-Khas are the **Hammans** or royal baths. Perfumed fountains played 24 hours in the first, which faced the river and a silver central jet gushed rose water. Dark green glass fitted the windows and the third bathroom was for hot baths. The apartments were separated by marble inlaid with precious stones.

Other buildings in the complex include **Samman Burj**, a tower with an octagonal dome, once coppered. The emperor saluted the rising sun here daily. *Aurangzeb* built the **Moti Masjid**, a small white marble mosque called Pearl Mosque, by the baths in 1662.

Fort Museums

The **Indian War Memorial Museum** is at the east side of *Chandni Chowk*. Established after World War 1, it has armoury, uniforms, stamps, coins and photographs. The **Museum of Archaeology** is in the *Mumtaz Mahal*. Small, it shows samples of life in Moghul times through manuscripts, art work, garments and weapons.

The musea close 15 minutes before the Fort which is open from 9 a.m. to 5 p.m. daily. There's a charge but admission is free Fridays. The war museum opens at 10 a.m. and is closed Friday.

Delhi

Son Et Lumiere

The history of India, particularly associated with the Red Fort and Delhi, is re-enacted in sound and light every evening. There are shows nightly in English and Hindi but times alter because of seasonal light. Book with the Government of India Tourist Office, (GITO) 88, Janpath. Tel: 32005, the Indian Tourist Development Corporation, (ITDC) L-Block, Connaught Place. Tel: 42336. Also at travel counters at the Ashok, Akbar, Janpath and some other hotels.(Ask at yours.)

Before exploring Old Delhi via Chandni Chowk, deviate to two quiet memorials, set behind the Red Fort on *Mahatma Gandhi Road*. The first and northerly one is **Shanti Vana** or the Forest of Peace. This tranquil wooded garden is where India's first Prime Minister *Jawaharlal Nehru* was cremated in 1964. His grandson Sanjay Gandhi was also cremated here at a columned platform by a pool in 1980. This place is called **Sanjay Samadhi**. And at *Shakti Sthala*, also by the complex, prime minister **Indira Gandi** was cremated following her assassination.

Further south is **Vijay Ghat**, a victory memorial at which India's second prime minister **Lal Bahadur Shastri** was cremated following his death in **Tashkent** during talks with Pakistan in 1966. His death, just after he had signed the peace treaty between the two countries, followed his major confrontation with Pakistan a year earlier.

At the southern edge of the memorial, cross *Mahatma Gandi Road* and proceed west until you reach *Ansari Road* which becomes *Netaji Subash Marg* (or road) when you head north. As you reapproach the Red Fort, you won't fail to miss on your left, Jama Masjid which is diagonally opposite it.

Jama Masjid

This is India's largest mosque, built over six years from 1644 by Emperor **Shah Jehan** to the design of *Ustad Khali*. It was the emperor's swansong and rivalled only by his architectural coup at *Fotehpursikri* (37 km west of Agra,) although son *Aurangzeb* finished it in 1658. Set on a rocky hill, it is also constructed of red sandstone but with alternating slabs of marble. Approached by three gateways, it has a 400 square metre courtyard reached by stone steps. The eastern gateway's gallery was reserved for royalty with marble seats set above sandstone slabs for the commoners. From here is a good view of the Red Fort. The prayer hall to the west, by which are two minarets, has three striped domes.

Women may not be permitted to climb the minaret unless they are in company with a responsible male 'family member.' There is a charge to ascend a minaret and also extra if you bring a camera with you. Daily, non Muslims are prohibited during prayer times of 12.30 p.m. to 2 p.m. This is the scene for mass prayers at most Muslim festivals.

> **INFOTIP:** At active temples and mosques, visitors are obliged to remove their shoes which are minded by an attendant for a small tip. At some Hindu and Jain temples, travellers wearing or carrying leather may be denied entrance so swap leather accessories for cotton, plastic or straw. At a Sikh temple, males and females must cover their heads.

Chandni Chowk

Continue north until you again reach Chandni Chowk. With the Red Fort on your right, turn left and you will see the **Digamber Jain Temple**. Next to it is the **Charity Bird Hospital**. It is surprising to some westerners that this institution exists. But the role of birds in the ecological system, carrying seeds, catching insects etc., is recognised in Delhi and injured birds are restored at the hospital which is actually part of the Jain Temple.

The **Digamber Jain Lal Mandir** is a temple built in 1656 and is colonnaded round its marble courtyard. The sanctuary's interior is painted, guilded and carved.

Be prepared for a crushing crowd in Chandni Chowk 24-hours a day. It is the main bazaar in old Delhi and will take some time to walk although a taxi won't proceed too much faster.

> **INFOTIP:** It could be fun to take a rickshaw, cycle powered. Establish the price first.

The bazaar begins with **Laipat Rai Market**. Be on the lookout for gold and silver jewellery bargains in this street.

Other buildings of interest in the street are the **Gauri Shanker Temple**, a marble and white sandstone place of Hindu worship containing idols of **Lord Shiva, Parvati, Lakshmi** and **Lord Krishna**. On the left side as you go west is the **Gurdwara Sisganj**, the place built by the Sihks to honour their guru **Tegh Bahadur** who was supposed to have been martyred here. Diagonally opposite is the **Bhagirath Palace**. On the same right-hand side is the Delhi Municipal Corporation and Town Hall. This building was erected in 1866. There is a western style fountain of red sandstone. By the police station is the **Sunchari**

Mosque of minarets and gilded domes from where *Nadir Shar*, who carted the Peaock Throne off to Iran, watched his army sacking the city.

Finally at the west end of Chandni Chowk is the **Fatehpuri Mosque** named after one of *Shah Jehan's* wives who had it built in 1650 of red sandstone and tiled with black and white marble. Its big courtyard is centred by a fountain.

If you continue further west, crossing *Shiradha Nand Marg*, the railway line and Qutab Road, the street becomes **Sadar Bazar Road** where you can shop in the colourful bazaar if you haven't bought enough in the winding maze of Chandni Chowk with its markets, fortune tellers and fascinations. The Sadar Bazar Railway Station is just north and you can catch a train for first New Delhi Station with its close access to **Pahar Ganj**, New Delhi's main bazaar or Minto Bridge Station which is very close to central Connaught Place.

But if you go north along Qutab Road, turn left into Boulevard Road then right at Rani Jhansi Marg, you will see the **Mutiny Memorial**, erected by the British to honour their dead from the Great Mutiny. Just north of it is Ashoka's Pillar (there are two in Delhi.)

Ashoka's Pillar

Approximately 10 metres high, this pillar was originally erected in 295 BC at *Firozabad* and was brought to Delhi in the middle of the 14th century by *Feroz Shah Tughlak*. When first seen by the British in the early 17th century, the pillar was topped by a gilded crescent and a glove, both of which were badly damaged by lightning a century later and were removed. The pillar was felled when a powder magazine exploded nearby in the mid 19th century but the British re-erected it in 1867.

Back on Qutab Road, proceed south until it becomes Chelmsford Road which leads directly into Connaught Place. This can be the base from which to enjoy more excursions.

Connaught Place

This immense shopping complex, containing most facilities the visitor needs, comprises two concentric circles with roads radiating out as spokewheels.

> **INFOTIP:** Check with GITO on the reliability of the stores offering to freight items to your home address.

There are colonnaded verandahs, a park with fountain, a car park and an air-conditioned market underground, called **Palika Bazaar**. It is somewhat dim and grubby but has anything the shopper wants. The circus-like complex was erected in 1931 to honour the visit to India of the Duke of Connaught.

Facilities include restaurants, hotels, cinemas, post office, some airline offices, the first class railway reservation office (opposite block K between radial Roads 4 and 5,) and the bus for the airport leaves from Block F, Radial Road 8. The Vayudoot airline office is close by. The eighth radial road soon becomes Janpath so if you need the help of the Government of India Tourist Office, continue south. You'll find it at number 88 on the left of the road.

The government emporia of most Indian States are located south west of Radial Road 2 on Baba Kharak Singh Marg. Goods are at fixed prices. (See shopping.)

Qutab Minar, Victory Tower

Delhi

Jantar Mantar Observatory

From Radial Road 1, stroll down till the street becomes re-named Sansad Marg or Parliament Street. Here you will find almost immediately the observatory built by **Maharajah Sawai Jai Singh** of **Jaipur**. It was commissioned in 1719 by Delhi's Moghul emperor to correct astronomical movements and revise calendars. Instead of constructing the observatory in brass, the Jaipur king used masonary material.

The result is an amazing collection of six lime-coated geometric structures aligned to longtitude, latitude, meridien and constellations set amid sculptured greenery and palm trees. The major structure is the vertical right-angled triangle, the **Samrat Yantra** or prince of sundials.

> **INFOTIP:** Addresses to various shops and agencies are given in alphabetical blocks. If you have appointments or wish to deal with known establishments, phone ahead first and ascertain which is the closest radial road. The radial roads number one to eight. This will save time.

Delhi

Raj Ghat

This is one of independent India's most sacred shrines, the final resting place of **Mahatma Gandhi** who was cremated on January 31, 1948, the day after the Father of the Nation was assassinated. Pilgrims visit constantly the simple, black-marbled platform on which Gandhi's last words '**He Ram**' are inscribed. Surrounded by green lawns, and trees planted by foreign heads of state, the shrine is enclosed in four walls.

> **INFOTIP:** Unlike some tourist offices, GITO on Janpath doesn't have a huge array of literature on display for people who drop in. So don't think you have come to the wrong place. Staff are most helpful and will discuss your needs and present you with literature when you sit down to discuss your plans.

The Ashoka Pillar

Delhi

Laxshmi Narayan Temple

The road that is 9 o'clock on the clockface of Connaught Place, between Radials Roads 2 and 3 (but fed by neither) is Bhagat Singh Marg. Follow it westwards, cross Ramakrishna Ashram Marg and you'll end up on Mandir Marg. On it, just left is the temple dedicated to the goddess of wealth, **Laxshmi** and her **Lord Vishnu**. Created just before World War II by a wealthy Hindu businessman and philanthropist **Raja Baldev Das Birla** (whose home became the Mahatma Gandhi Museum,) the temple includes paintings and sculptures which reflect, through their Jaipur artists, the great teachings of Hinduism.

Just north of Connaught Place on Chelmsford Road and opposite the New Delhi Railway Station is Market or Main Bazaar Road. Here is a proliferation of low-budget hotels in the most central of locations.

The next parallel-right road leading north from Connaught Place is Vivekanand Marg. Take it until you reach Jawaharlal Nehru Road and turn right. You'll locate a camping ground here. If you have not seen the **Turkman Gate** or the **Delhi Gate**, go one further major street north and turn also right into Asaf Ali Road. Both roads, heading east, culminate in Mahatma Gandhi Road and you'll see **Raj Ghat** directly ahead, set by the riverbank.

Mahatma Gandhi Memorial Museum

Diagonally opposite the Raj Ghat is the **Gandhi National Museum** and **Library**. Closed on Monday, it is otherwise open from 9.30 am to 5.30 pm. Naturally devoted to displays on Mahatma Gandhi's life, the museum has Sunday film shows about the great leader. These are shown at 4 pm in Hindi and 5 pm in English. Entrance is free. Inquiries: Tel. 274746.

Feroz Shah Kotla Ashoka's Pillar

Further south are the ruins of **Ferozabad**, which was the fifth of Delhi's historical old cities. It is also known as **Kushak-i-Feroshah**. It was built in 1354 by the Emperor **Feroz Shah Tuglak**. The citadel was bounded by a 12 metre high wall. Not much remains of three palaces, eight mosques and hunting lodges. But the enclosure includes the **Ashoka Pillar** which is a monolithic, tapering sandstone pillar which dates back to the third century BC. It was brought from the State of Haryana to Delhi. On the pillar are edicts and messages of goodwill and peace - being the first of Ashoka's commands to be deciphered in 1937 by **James Princep**. This translation became the

Delhi

previous missing link in the **Brahmi script.**

Proceed to the end of the block and turn right. Then, turn right again into Bahadur Shah Zafar Marg. On the right is the Gandhi Memorial Hall.

International Dolls Museum

Next in the Nehru Building is the International Dolls Museum which is open 10 am to 6 pm every day except Monday. It houses a fascinating collection of more than 6000 dolls from more than 80 countries. A large proportion of the dolls are from India and there is a special display featuring all of the traditional costumes in the nation.

Diagonally opposite the museum is the Foreign Post Office.

Victory Tower

Throne at the Red Ford

Khuni Darwaza (Kabuli)

In the same street on the left is an imposing grey, stone gateway, the only remains of a city encouraged to spread towards the south-east by Sher Shah Suri. The gate was the horrific sight where, during the 1857 **Indian Mutiny**, the British executed the sons and other male relatives of the last **Mughal Emperor, Bahadur Shah Zafar**, after whom this main thoroughfare is named. Directly ahead is the Delhi Gate.

If you now turn around completely and head south, you'll see that this road divides into three after crossing the railway line at **Tilak Bridge Station**. Just before the bridge at left is the Foreigners' Registration Office. Take the left fork after the bridge or Mathura Road for several attractions but if you want to go directly to the India Gate, opt for the middle street, Tilak Marg.

Crafts Museum

A fair distance down Mathura Road on the left is the Crafts Museum in the Exhibition grounds (**Aditi Pavilion.**) Set up in a village-styled complex, with free admission, the museum displays ceramics, brass and copper ware, wooden and texile goods made in the traditional Indian manner. Open 9.30 am to 4.30 pm, it is closed Sundays.

Continuing south, the Purana Qila or Old Fort is also on the left.

Purana Quila (Old Fort)

The Purana Qila is believed to be the ancient, legendary city of **Indraprastha**, the first of Delhi's seven cities, named **Dinpanah** by **Emperor Humayan**. Mentioned in the epic **Mahabtara**, it was the city in which the Pandava brothers, who were sun-worshippers, lived.

Hugely walled, it has three entrances. The northern entrance is called **Talaqi Darwaja** which translates into **Forbidden Gate**. The fort's archaeological finds have indicated it was built originally in the third century BC with additions and re-construction taking place up till Moghul times. Noteable was the *Moghul Emperor Humayan*. He was defeated by Sher Shah, the Afghan ruler who reigned until Humayan regained the throne and India in 1545. **Sher Shah** had knocked down the fortifications first constructed by Humayan and his citadel's ramparts extend for about 2 km in an oblong shape with corner bastions and in the west wall.

A combination of Hindu-Muslim architecture, the fort includes a mosque built by Sher Shah Suri. Just beyond it south is the **Sher Mandal**, an octagonal 1th century pavilion built by Sher Shah as a house of pleasure. Legend holds that Humayan heard the call to prayers at the mosque and, in his hurry, fell on the steps of Sher Mandal. His injuries proved fatal. There is a viewing platform behind Sher Mandal above the archaeologists' digs but the most important finds are housed in a small museum close by. If you exit by the south gate, you will face the national zoological gardens.

> **INFOTIP:** On excursions, take bottled mineral water with you. When buying it, check the seal has not been broken. While you can buy bottled soft drinks in many villages and towns, sometimes they are unavailable. Don't take ice in your drink. The water may not have been previously boiled.

Delhi

Delhi Zoo

The zoo is renowned most for its white tigers and birds. Opening hours are 8 a.m. to 6 p.m. in summer and 9 a.m. to 5 p.m. in winter. There is an entrance fee but children under five are free.

Continue south and Mathura Road is intersected with Dr. Zakir Hussain Road. On your right is The **Oberoi Hotel**, a grand place in which to stop for refreshments. And it also houses one of the finest collections of 18th and 19th century art in India, plus contemporary work by such artists as UN Peace Medal winner, **Amar Nath Sehgal**. There is art of India and also original, international works displayed such as 19th century Chinese watercolours in its rooftop Szechuan restaurant, Taipan.

Set in large grounds by the Delhi Golf Course. The property borders Lodi Road to the south and it is here, when meeting Lodi, that you should turn left to meet again Mathura Road which has bled down from Dr. Zakir Hussain. Travel directly east along Lodi and you will discover Humayan's Tomb.

Humayan's Tomb

Bordered by ruined walls but still-standing ornamental gateways, the tomb of the unfortunate Humayan was erected by his senior wife **Haji Begum** as one of the earliest, if not the first, examples of Moghal architecture,

Delhi

Humayan's Tomb

leading other monuments in style, including the **Taj Mahal**. The tomb's architect, the Persian **Mirak Mirza Ghiyas**, designed it as an original trend-setting, tomb-garden complex and it was finished in 1565, nine years after the second Moghul emperor's death.

Entry is via four gateways and along stone-paved paths through formalized gardens which have been divided into four squares. Domed over arched entrances, the 43-metre high mausoleum has a central octagonal cenotaph in which the emperor and the Moghul princes **Dara Shokoh, Alamgir II** and **Bahadur ShahII** are buried. There are Afghan to Lodi dynasty tombs also in the gardens. An entrance fee applies, except for Sundays when it is free.

Now go back across Mathura Road diagonally south west for Hazrat Nizamuddin Aulia.

Hazrat Nizamuddin Aulia

This is the shrine to the Moslem saint, the **Sheikh Nizamuddin Christi** who died in 1325 and is known to followers of the faith the world over. For centuries, a mediaeval village existed around the tomb and it became a burial ground of Muslim nobility, including **Jahanara**, the daughter of **Shah Jehan**, the poet **Mirza Ghalib** and a disciple of Nizamuddin, **Amir Khusrau**.

Originally surrounded by four sides of verandah round a

square, marble chamber, the main shrine has been gradually renovated and the roof topped with an octagonal drum, a black, vertically-striped dome and the grave is surrounded by a marble balustrade.

The shrine is accessible from Nizamuddin Railway Station which is also the one closest to Humayun's Tomb.

You are now almost back on Lodi Road if you face north. Turn left into Lodi Road and then right into Archbishop Makarios Marg bordering the golf links and the Oberoi Hotel for a look at Embassy Row.

Tibet House

Just down from the Oberoi at 16 Jor Bagh off Lodi Road is Tibet House, an interesting museum displaying treasures smuggled out of Tibet at the time the **Dalai Lhama**, threatened by the in-coming Chinese, left his country. There are also Tibetan crafts for sale in a separate shop. Closed Sundays, the museum is open 10 a.m. to 1 p.m. and 2.30 p.m. to 6 p.m. Tel: 611515.

Lodi Gardens

If you continue west along Lodi Road, you will reach Amrita Shergil Marg. These two streets border the Lodi Gardens which are the largest in central Delhi. Once known as **Lady Willingdon Park**, the gardens are a delightful place to stroll to see waterfalls and springs, the people of Delhi at leisure and also monuments from the Lodi Dynasty. Well maintained, the gardens include the tomb of Sikander Lodi on a rise in the north-west section. Built in 1518 by Ibrahim Lodi, his son, the tomb is octagonal, has a mosque and a Persian-style double dome. It is decorated with Hindu motifs. **Ibrahim** and **Mubarak Shah** and **Mohammad Shah** are also buried here. The design of the latter's tomb provided the inspiration to the architect of Humayun's tomb, which, of course, led to the creative thought behind the Taj Mahal.

Safdarjang's Tomb

Return to Lodi Road, where there are more embassies on the south side, then head west again and you will happen on Safdarjang's Tomb completed in 1754 by **Nawab Suji-ud-Daula** for his father who was the second **Nawab of Oudh** and the Emperor Mohammad Shah's Prime Minister. Two-storeyed with polygonal towers on the corners, the red and buff sandstone tomb with white marble panelled reliefs is domed and is one of the final reflections of Moghul architecture to be erected before the demise of the empire. The Archaeological Survey of India has devoted the southern pavilion to a museum.

Entrance to the tomb is free on Fridays, but otherwise there is a charge. The tomb is adjacent to the small airport of the same name at which Indira Gandhi's son, Sanjay, was killed in 1980. Here, too, some Vayudoot flights to and from other parts of India take off and land.

India Gate

This airport is home to the Delhi Gliding Club and the Flying Club. North of the tomb is Delhi Racecourse with the Delhi Racing Club and the Riding Club.

Diagonally opposite and heading north-east is Prith Viraj Road. This becomes Shah Jahan Road at the point where Man Singh Road leads off to the north. At number 1 of this latter road is the **Taj Mahal Hotel** in which suites are decorated with priceless objets d' art. The hotel has an elegant rooftop restaurant specializing in Italian cuisine.

If you continue north along Shah Jahan Road, you cannot fail to miss the India Gate.

India Gate

The **Duke of Connaught** laid the foundation stone of this triumphal arch and, on completion, this all-India War Memorial commemorated the more than 90,000 Indian soldiers who lost their lives during the Great War of 1914-18. The inscription on the India Gate reads:

'To the dead of the Indian Armies who fell honoured in France and Flanders, Mesopatamia and Persia, East Africa, Gallipoli and elsewhere in the near and far east. And in sacred memory also of those whose names are recorded and who fell in India or the north-west frontier and during the Third Afghan War.' (1919.)

At a height of 42 metres, the gate was topped by a stone bowl in which an eternal flame to the **Unknown Soldier** has been burning since 1971. The India Gate was officially inaugurated in 1931. It is floodlit at night and is at the eastern end of Raj Path. The India Gate is opposite the **National Stadium** to the east and fed by 11 roads.

South of the Gate in one of six garden areas surrounding it, is a children's park.

Raj Path, In Its Steps

Raj Path, or the grand thoroughfare which extends from India Gate to **Rashtrapati Bhavan** and the **Mughal Gardens** in a straight line from east to west contains most of India's most important federal government buildings. Raj Path also runs parallel to two other major roads of four different names and the impression is one of enormous space and dignity.

First place of interest on the left after leaving India Gate is Vigyan Bhavan.

Vigyan Bhavan

This is a huge complex which is a specially-designed convention- conference centre of halls, meeting rooms, offices and extra facilities which are congregated around a vast, central auditorium. It can seat 1100 delegates and on either side two conference rooms will each accommodate 300 more. Five other meeting rooms each have a capacity of 80 people. This distinguished building, its facade modelled on the Buddhist architectural pattern, has as a feature a sacred pipal leaf fashioned out of marble. It has its own peaceful garden and was built in 1956. The complex was used for the seventh non-aligned Summit of 1983. This, at that time, was the largest meeting of heads of State at any international gathering.

Deviate just left into Janpath to see the treasures of the National Museum.

The National Museum

This museum is a modern building which accommodates rare, world-famous artifacts gouged from the excavations of the ancient **Indus Valley civilization**, some believed to date from 3000 BC. There are impressive sculptures from the **Mauryan** and **Sunga** periods between the third and second centuries BC and the **Kushan** and **Satavana** period between the first and third centuries. Other exhibits highlight the bronzes of the south **Indian Chola** era and also murals, clothing and miniatures from the **Vijayanagar** period in southern India.

While entrance fees are made weekdays when there are film shows, admission at weekends is free. Closed Mondays, this interesting museum is otherwise open between 10 am and 5 pm.

History buffs should proceed across Raj Path from the museum to discover on the left hand side the **National Archives of India**.

Further west along Raj Path on either side of the road are located the buildings of the Secretariat, north and south blocks. But before you look to either side, deviate at **Vijay Chowk**, formerly known as the Great Place, for a peek-a-boo at Parliament House.

Sansad Bhavan
Parliament House

Circular, (171 metres in diameter) colonnaded (144 columns of more than eight metres height) and impressive, Parliament House was opened in 1927 by the then Governor-General of India, **Lord Irwin**. Three main chambers radiate from the central hall which is high domed with fine oak panelled walls. The Constitution of India in its original hand-written form is in the parliamentary library. Chambers are separated by gardens and fountains and special permission is needed by visitors to inspect the whole complex.

If you wish you can continue diagonally north along Sansad Marg (Parliament Street,) which leads directly back to Connaught Place. Alternatively, retrace your steps back to Raj Path and turn right.

The Secretariat Complex

Proceeding west, the buildings to your right are the North Block, while the South Block is on the left. The complex was designed by **Herbert Baker** and each block is entered via an arched gate with domed pavilions. These feature frescoes and murals. Each block is four-storeyed.

Delhi

The Prime Minister's offices along with those of the Defence Minister and the Minister For External Affairs are in the South Block. The North Block includes the Finance Ministry and the Union Ministry.

Rashtrapati Bhavan

You will now be facing Raisini Hill on which stands the palatial Rashtrapati Bhavan. Formerly the palace of the British Viceroys of India and first occupied in 1929, it is now the Presidential Palace. Its last British occupant, Lord Louis Mountbatten employed a staff of several hundred Indian servants to maintain the palace and its beautiful grounds of more than 140 hectares. The architect was **Edwin Lutyens**. The palace includes huge courts, pillared porticos, magnificent staircases, marbled vestibules and is crowned by an impressive dome.

In the **Durbar** and **Ashoka Halls**, ceremonial functions are conducted. The palace is the setting for the swearing in of the Prime Minister and other Union ministers of the government when the central cabinet is constituted following an election.

The beautiful **Moghul Gardens** set beside the palace are open to the public in February. At other times, tourist passes will be issued by GITO at 88 Janpath or permission to enter can be gained from the Military Secretary to the President of India at Rashtrapati Bhavan.

Now, cross Raj Path and, proceeding south, get into Dalhousie Road which runs parallel to Raj Path. Turn left into South Avenue which leads to the Nehru Memorial Museum.

Nehru Memorial Museum

This museum is actually on **Teen Murti** Marg which is fed by South Avenue. It was originally the home of the British Commander-in-Chief of India during the latter years of the Raj. It became the official residence of **Pandit Nehru**, India's first Prime Minister, in 1948 and its exhibits are memorabilia of his life and work. It also is a library housing more than 50,000 books and periodicals. Closed on Mondays, the museum is open from 10 am to 5 pm on all other days. Admission is free, but if you attend the sunset sound and light show, '**Tryst With Destiny**,' there is a small charge. The son et lumiere shows are not conducted year round, so phone to check. Tel: 3015333.

Proceed south-west down Teen Murti Marg, turn left into Kautilya Marg and continue until reaching Niti Marg. Almost on the corner of this intersection and set on a small hill amid large grounds is the **Ashok Hotel**. This is the five-

Delhi

star flagship of the Indian Tourist Development Corporation's Ashok hotel chain which offers special holiday packages to foreign visitors in various parts of India in Ashok hotels.

The hotel has some excellent restaurants, including two which feature top Frontier and Moghlai fare. It also has Delhi's only totally Japanese restaurant - The Tokyo - which has authentic specialties served at either traditional Japanese or western-style tables.

If you now continue south on Niti Marg, you will pass Nehru Park on your left. It includes a swimming pool.

At the end of the park, where it is crossed by Satya Marg, Niti Marg sweeps to the right, and just across its intersection with Shanti Path, you will find the Rail Transport Museum on your left. If you are arriving by train, the nearest station to the museum is **Chanakyapuri**.

Shikaras and Houseboats

Delhi

Rail Transport Museum

India has a marvellous history of steam trains and this is reflected in the exhibits of this large property. There are nearly five hectares laid with railway track and visitors will see about 30 vintage locomotives, the earliest dating to 1855 and still in working order. If you can't get a seat on the famous **Palace On Wheels** which tours out of Delhi through Rajasthan, come to this museum for a comprehensive glimpse into the past. There is a small admission charge and you must pay an extra fee if you wish to take photographs of the exhibits. The museum is closed on Monday, otherwise open from 9.30 am to 1 pm and from 1.30 pm to 5 pm. Tel: 611803.

The next few attractions are so widespread in the south of Delhi that it would be inconceivable to attempt to walk. It is suggested that you take a taxi from Satya Marg which, incidentally, is at the bottom of the Chanakyapuri Diplomatic Enclave.

Diplomatic Enclave

This district of most diplomatic missions either side of the wide **Shanti Path** (or Road of Peace,) was named after a minister in the court of **Emperor Chandragupta**. Chanakyapuri was the first to write a treatise on how to organize affairs of State. The American Embassy, designed by **Edward Stone**, is opposite the Australian Embassy on Shanti Marg. The impressive American facility is open to the public.

Direct your driver from Shanti Marg to turn right and south down the long Africa Avenue until you reach park lands at the intersection of Harsukh Marg. The **Delhi Lawn Tennis Stadium** is almost on the corner. This large, open area includes a deer park, picnic hut and, in the south, a rose garden. Almost in the centre is Hauz Khas.

Inside Red Ford

Delhi

The Qutab Minar (Tower)

Dominating this southern area of Delhi and visable for several kilometres, the country's highest stone tower is 73 metres tall. The base is 14.5 metres in diameter tapering to 2.5 metres over five distinct storeys. These are believed to have risen at one stage to seven storeys in height. The first three sections are in red sandstone followed by marble and sandstone. The tower was begun by **Qutab-ud-din Aibak** as a celebration of victory over **Rajput** forces of the **Chauhan king** in 1192. It was finally completed by his successors and in 1368 Feroz Shah Tughlak added two more storeys with cupola. The tower was damaged by earthquake but restored early in the 19th century. Each storey has ornamental inscriptions from the Koran. The tower had the double purpose of being a watchtower and a minaret for the muezzin to call the faithful to prayer. Visitors can ascend to the first storey in groups of four for a small fee.

Quwwat-ul-Islam Mosque

Just below the Qutab Minar is a mosque believed to be India's earliest. Its name translates into 'Might of Islam' and it was started by *Qutab-ud-din Aibak* on the site of the Hindu temple known as **Vishnu Mandia**. Hindu decorations on the foundations were concealed with ornamentation and text from the Koran but time has revealed some of them. The rectangular mosque was built from material taken from 27 surrounding Hindu temples. Carved pillars stand in five rows. Two prayer rooms for women were added and also extra additions and changes were made by the emperors **Altmish and Ala-ud- din**.

The Iron Pillar

In the centre of the remains of the mosque's courtyard is one of the wonders of India's long civilization - a nine metre high pillar of cast iron, so pure that it has never rusted in its estimated age of approximately 2000 years. There is debate among academics on when the pillar was erected. Some say that it was in the last years of the 9th century while others consider it was cast in the reign of **Chandra Gupta II** a ruler of the **Gupta Dynasty** in the 4th century. Whatever its origins, the purity of the iron has amazed modern metallurgical experts. Some authorities believe the pillar was originally cast in the city of **Indraprasath** at the time of the epic **Mahabharata**, then moved to Bihar before being transported to Delhi to be erected before the Vishnu Mandir temple by the Rajput king,

Delhi

Anangpal Tomar early in the 11th century. This king is named in an inscription on the pillar.

The most puzzling of Indian monuments, when ancient effigies such as the Colossus of Rhodes and giant Buddhas were fashioned from metals welded together in sections, the Iron Pillar still stands in the 20th century as a technological enigma.

There is an incomplete tower of 27 metres built by **Ala-ud-din** as a second victory tower but it remains as it was on his death.

Just outside the western boundary of the complex is **Adham Khan's** tomb built by **Akbar The Great** in 1526. It was constructed in the Lodi style of tomb architecture. Also nearby are other tombs of the last of the Delhi kings.

To the north of this tomb is the **Jogmaya Temple**, said to be dedicated to **Lord Krishna's** sister, **Jogmaya**. It was built in 1857.

Rajastham Cameleer

Delhi

Hauz Khas

This is a huge tank, now in ruins, and formerly the water supply for Delhi's second city, **Siri**, when it was built in 1305. The reservoir originally covered more than 30 hectares. In the area is the tomb of **Feroz Shah Tughlak** and also buried there are his son, **Nasir-ud-din Mohammed Shah** and his grandson, **Sikandar Lodi**. Outside the tomb are more of the burial places of **Amirs** from this era. There are remains of a college where students were accommodated in cells so designed to be warm in winter and cool in summer. Hauz Khas is open from sunrise to sunset daily.

If you don't come to Hauz Khas for its ruins, drop in for an offbeat shopping area - bazaars which have sprung up over the years and shops more recently established by business people offering western wares to compliment the ethnic. Here is a combination of modern and mediaeval and the buyer benefits in the one curiously combined village.

Africa Avenue runs into Palam Road. You will have turned left into this road to get to Hauz Khas. Sri Aurobindo Marg crosses Palam Road. Turn right and head south for the Qutab Minar Complex.

Qutab Minar

Qutab Minar Complex

The complex comprising a group of monuments which include the Qutab Minar, India's highest tower, is more than 14 km south of New Delhi. Because there is so much to see, it would be wise to devote at least a half day or take a guided tour which includes it. You can also reach the complex from Connaught Place by taking a public bus which leaves from the Delhi Transport Corporation building.

The buildings include interesting remains from the beginnings of Muslim domination in India and are excellent examples of the architecture of the time, dating from the 12th century. **Tomb of Imam Zamin**.

Outside the main entrance gateway, the **Alai Darwaza**, is the tomb of Imam Zamin which was built at the time of the Mughal emperor Humayun. Imam Zamin was of the Chishtian sect and came to Delhi from Turkistan at the time of *Sikandar Lodi*. He was appointed Imam which was the highest official in the **Quww-ul-Islam** mosque. The domed sandstone tomb featuring polished stucco is square in shape.

Tughlakabad

On leaving the Qutab Minar Complex, travel east along the Mehrauli Badarpur Road towards Badapur and you will reach Tughlakabad which was the third city of Delhi and is approximtaley 20 km south east of New Delhi.

It was a major fort built on a rocky emminence in 1324 by **Ghais-ud-din Tughlak** with 13 gates piercing its massive walls. Today, the ruins are a sad reminder of this huge fort's former glory. Tradition has it that Tughlakabad was built in only two years - an impressive feat if true. There is a legend that the fort was cursed by a saint, **Nizam-ud-din** who quarrelled with Ghais-ud-din because the ruler conscripted workers who were building the saint's shrine at the time. Nizam-ud-din's curse must have been pretty potent as the king was murdered only a year later on a short journey between the fort and Delhi.

Ghais-ud-Din Tughlak's tomb is located just outside the ruined walls in a lake.

> **INFOTIP:** As you prepare to leave Delhi on short side trips, ascertain, if you are flying, whether or not your aircraft will be an airbus. Indira Gandhi International Airport is connected to the domestic airport but there are different entrances. There is also a special entry for airbus passengers so if you are travelling by taxi, know whether to direct it to domestic or airbus terminals.

KASHMIR

Vales of Awesome Beauty

Kashmir. Even the sound of the word evokes romance, thoughts of mystic beauty and images of the daunting, snowcapped Himalayas reflecting in lakes and slow moving stretches of river.

But India's most northerly State, which sits like an ornamental bow on the top of the nation which roughly resembles the head of a shorn sheep, is actually called **Jammu** and Kashmir, abbreviated to J & K. Jammu is really the south while Kashmir is a valley in the bosom of the Himalayas which, legend holds, was once a lake as extensive as an inland sea. After most of the lake water had drained, the demon believed to live here was killed by Brahma's godson **Kashap** and the Hindi goddess **Parvati** who dropped him fatally on to a mountain which, now, is

Kashmiri Beauty

Takht Sulaiman, the hill against which **Srinagar**, the capital of the State, is set.

It is Kashmir, the vale with its lakes, streams and mountains, glorious in all seasons, that most people want to see. Several continue trekking or by air to Ladakh, the northeast Tibetan plateau and another region within J & K, more Tibetan than today's Chinese-dominated Tibet.

The visitors come for an unparalled experience of living on a houseboat on Srinagar's **Lakes Dal** or **Nagin** in the relaxed, often pampered, manner of the British who initiated the houseboat concept because they were not permitted to buy land to build holiday homes in what was then a princely state and not part of the India overtaken by the English. Experience of a good houseboat is unforgettable.

Kashmir

Moghul Gardens

Travellers come for eye-widening scenic beauty, trekking and sights of the monuments and gardens of the **Grand Moghuls** from Emperor Ashok through to Emperor Jehangir whose dying words were: *'Kashmir, only Kashmir...'*

They are attracted by the forested hill stations not far from Srinagar, cool in summer, some offering snow sports in winter. And the whole State includes most of India's most exciting adventure sports and experiences.

Srinagar is an ideal extension from Delhi for at least three days. It is accessible from Delhi in 65 minutes by air bus. Other flights stop at **Jammu** and **Amritsar** and take much longer. You can reach Jammu by train from Delhi, (inevitably an overnight trip,) then connect with a morning bus from Jammu or bus the 876 km from Delhi to Srinagar.

> **INFOTIP:** New arrivals at he airport must register at the Foreigners' Registration desk which is just inside the terminal. It's only a table so don't miss it as you move across to collect your baggage.

Buses arrive at the J & K Tourist Reception Centre, just up from Dal Gate in the heart of town. Opposite are the tourism offices where there is modest accommodation in rooms and dormitories, two restaurants (one good Chinese,) post office and offices for tours, transport, and accommodation including houseboats.

Similar offices are at the airport, about 14 km from the city which can be reached by bus or taxi.

Kashmir

Despite what some other travel guides recommend, **Lake Dal**, although pretty and excitingly adjacent to town, has become quite polluted in recent years. If this bothers you, chose a houseboat at the far end of this lake or opt for scenic **Lake Nagin**, so-called the **Jewel in the Ring** and 8 km via a causeway by car from Srinagar or a shikara ride across, then a taxi ride into town. Another alternative is to glide by gondola-like shikara along the canals which connect Dal with Nagin - a must of an excursion in any case.

It is this intersecting network of three lakes (add **Wular Lake**,) canals, river and floating gardens which gives Srinagar its reputation as being the **Venice of the East**. Some call it the **Amsterdam of India**, and indeed, many of the old-style Kashmiri houses, leaning as if they are about to topple into the water, at least bear this resemblance to Holland's capital.

But the architecture, with its gingerbread house-like ornamentations and carvings and steep roofs, is distinctly different. So too are the people. Most men wear the **pheran**, a loose, full coat over baggy trousers and wear astrakan caps. Women, the majority, like the men, Muslim, wear traditional Kashmiri pants and long tops. You will see many in black with their faces fully veiled.

Now, let's start your Srinagar experience, commencing at Dal Gate. Travelling north-east, you can ride on Lake Dal past the greatest conglomeration of houseboats and one series of floating gardens by shikara, or go by taxi. To the right you will see Shankracharya Hill.

Kashmir

Shankracharya Temple

About 300 metres above the city, this hill is also known as **Takht-i-Sulaiman**, so-named because Solomon's transport to heaven, according to legend, was supposed to rest here. It is site of a temple first built by Emperor Ashok's son, **Juluka** about 200 BC. A low wall and plinth remains of the old temple. The present structure is believed to have been built in the reign of **Emperor Jehangir** by an anonymous devout Hindu. From the temple are wonderful views of the valley and the snow-clad peaks of the **Pir Pangal Range**.

The drive to the top of the hill is about 5 km from town and a nice time to ascend is just before sunset.

Proceeding along the banks of Dal Lake via Boulevard Rd, you will pass **Nehru Park** which is an island on the left, then bathing boats from which one can swim. Further along is the **Oberoi Palace Hotel** with its gardens sloping down towards the lake.

To reach it by road, take Gupkar Rd. from Dal Gate, if you are staying or wish to call in for a look at this former Maharajah's palace and a good Kashmiri meal.

Back on the Boulevard or Lake Dal you will see the extensive gardens of the Hotel Contaur Lake View. Then, 11 km from the city on the lake banks is Nishat Bagh.

Shankaracharya Temple

Kashmir

Nishat Bagh (Gardens)

With the **Zabarwan Mountains** as its backdrop, the 'Garden Of Bliss' was designed by the brother of Nur Jehan, **Asaf Khan**, in 1633. The vast garden has a wonderful lake view and also a view of **Pir Panjal Range** to the west.

Passing the Gupta Ganga Temple, you will soon happen upon the renowned Shalimar Gardens.

Shalimar Bagh (Gardens)

The site was selected by **Emperor Jehangir** in 1619 as Kashmir's most idyllic. The emperor, reputedly with a harem of 800, had been a violent drinker and opium addict until, in middle age, he fell in love with a cultured Persian widow. She became **Empress Nur Jehan** - *'Light of the World'* - on their marriage. He rejected his bad ways and created the garden as an abode of love. It has pools, fountains, pavilions, trees and flowers set in four terraced levels.

Their love story is re-enacted during May to September in son et lumiere performances. The English show begins at 9 p.m. There is a charge.

To the right of the gardens is a road leading to Harwan, 19 km from the city.

Harwan

On a hill south of this village archaeologists have discovered pavements from the Buddhist period. These ancient tile pavements are ornamented and reveal the manner of dress of the people of that time. Turkoman caps, baggy trousers, turbans and big earrings reflect the influences of central Asia. If you do not go to Harwan, you can see samples of the tiles in the Srinagar Museum.

Returning to the Shalimar Gardens, you can continue by road in a large loop which will culminate in your being on the west bank of Lake Dal. It is a delightful though fairly lengthy drive but you will pass through interesting villages with busy markets and through lovely land punctuated by forest and farmland.

Naseem Bagh (Gardens)

Although the gardens are now used by the Engineering College and University, they are interesting for having been laid out by Akbar in 1586. The Nagin Club is just south of the gardens.

Kashmir

Break by a Canal

> **INFOTIP:** For a fun souvenir, dress up as a Mughlai emperor or empress for a small fee to the costume-providers in the park and have a companion take your photograph.

Hazratbal Mosque

This mosque, opposite **Nishat Bagh**, is relatively new and has a wonderful view of the lake and the mountains beyond. Open to the public on special occasions (ask of J & K Tourism,) the mosque houses a sacred hair of the Prophet Mohammad and is regarded by followers as a shrine.

You are now only 9 km from downtown and almost on the banks of **Lake Nagin**. However, you might like to explore this area at another time, so let us retrace our route to the city via the **Shalimar Gardens**.

There is a road which branches away from Lake Dal almost opposite **Rupa Lank** (Gold Island.) This leads through the hills to **Nehru Memorial Park** and then continues south-east to Cheshma Shahi.

Cheshma Shahi

This terraced Moghul garden was created by **Shah Jehan** in 1632 and contains a cool spring. In recent years, it has been extended and developed into a tourist village with shops and lodgings. Again, there are lovely Lake Dal views and the gardens are lit at night. There is a small admission charge.

Now proceed back inland towards the Oberoi Palace Hotel.

Pari Mahal

On your left, the Pari Mahal is a former Buddhist monastery which was translated by the eldest son of Shah Jehan, **Dara Shikoh**, into a school of astrology. Also overlooking Lake Dal with six terraces of garden before it, the Pari Mahal is floodlit at night. The building is also known as the Palace of Fairies.

From here, it is just a short drive back to downtown **Srinagar**.

Just south of Dal Gate is Maulana Azad Road. On the right hand corner is a golf links and opposite on the left is the **Tourist Reception Centre**. Down this road are several restaurants and cafes. It runs parallel to Sherwani Road, then, The Bund on the **River Jhelum**. At the end of Maulana Azad Rd., cross the Badshah Bridge. The Old Secretariat building will be just ahead and just beyond is the bustling **Central Market**.

Now, from the bridge, curve your way south on the opposite river bank and you will reach the Museum and Library.

Shri Pratap Singh Museum

This museum and library is situated on **Lal Mandi** and is open between 10 a.m. and 5 p.m. Entrance is free for views of Kashmiri exhibits and the **Harwan** pavement tiles. Also there are rare Buddhist antiquities from Tibet, Ladakh and central Asia and sculptures, paintings, coins, clay seals, bronzes and terracotta artifacts. It is closed Wednesdays and Government holidays. Just a few blocks further on is a silk-weaving factory. You can get back to Dal Gate by crossing **Zero Bridge** just down from this factory.

From Dal Gate again, take a **shikara** on a rather rambling but fascinating ride north along a canal connecting with the Jhelem River, first to see Shah Hamdan Mosque and then, Pather Masjid mosque.

Shah Hamdan Mosque

One of the city's oldest mosques, the wooden Shah Hamdan, built in the late 1300s, was later burnt down twice. Now with a roof like a pyramid soaring upwards into a spire, it has very fine papier mache work on its walls and ceilings.

> **INFOTIP:** While this mosque is supposedly inaccessible to non-Muslims, depending on who is in charge, you may be able to enter to see the papier mache work for a tip. Just opposite is the Pather Masjid.

Pather Masjid

You are now in the heart of the old city and facing a stone mosque which its builder, **Nur Jehan**, created specifically for Shia sect Muslims to pray. Leave your skikara here to cross the bridge and pass the tomb of **Zain-ul- Abidin**. The tomb is that of the son of **Sultan Sikander** and reflects the Persian style of architecture from that period. Just ahead is Jami Masjid.

Jami Masjid

Made of wood, and built first by Sultan Sikandar in 1400, then enlarged by his son, whose tomb you have just passed, this mosque was burnt down three times and each time reconstructed. This mosque, with scores of tree trunk pillars supporting the roof, is of **Indo-Saracenic** design. There is an inner courtyard. You are now within a short distance of Hari Parbat Fort.

Hari Parbat Fort

If you do not wish to go to the trouble of gaining permission to visit this imposing fort at the top of a winding road which ascends the **Sharika Hill**, return the meandering way back by shikara to Dal Gate, then, directly north through a canal to **Lake Nagin** (which would still be Lake Dal if it had not been separated by a causeway.) On the south-west shore you can stop, enjoy the Kashmiri tea your shikara man will prepare for you and, a packed lunch if you have arranged with your hotel or houseboat staff for this break to be made. Towering above you will be the Fort and on and by the lake you will see Kashmir's fascinating birdlife and colourful water traffic.

The reason why permission is needed to visit the fort is that it is regarded as sacred by the Hindus. You will see

Kashmir

almond orchards surrounding the hill around which **Akbar** built a defensive wall between 1592 and 1598. The fort was built by an Afghan governor, **Atta Mohammad Khan** in the 18th century. To gain permission to enter, contact the J & K Director of Tourism or the State Archaeological Department, Lal Mandi Square, just opposite the Tourist Reception Centre.

Srinagar's night life is not exactly glittering but, because there is no prohibition, there are several bars around town. Nightlife is centred around the larger hotels and the houseboats. One of the pleasant surprises of a houseboat stay can be the interesting people you meet if you have not booked out the two to three bedroomed vessel with dining and living rooms for yourself or your party. (There's no TV or radio but relaxing in the evening on the lake facing balcony and bargaining or conversing with passing shikara-people is quiet entertainment.) Fellow guests can range from international celebrities to interesting travellers of the world.

> **INFOTIP:** For romance, there's nothing like a night shikara ride. The boats accommodate three to five but two can stretch out in utter comfort. There's a legend that if you cruise the lakes by shikara with a full moon lighting the tops of the Himalayas, you are sure to return. One of the authors of this guide can attest to the legend's truth.

A helpful houseboat owner may introduce you to other guests staying on adjoining boats. In deluxe and A class houseboats, guests frequently enjoy a choice of national cuisines and a Kashmiri **wazwan** (or traditional) meal may be able to be arranged on shore.

> **INFOTIP:** Unlike hotels, Srinagar's houseboats do not supply liquor and it's aboput the only commodity shikaramen don't bring to your sun deck-balcony. But there are plenty of places in town where you can buy your own to party on the lakes.

A not to be missed excursion from Srinagar if time allows is the 60 km journey into the '**Meadow of Flowers**' - **Gulmarg** - India's skiing capital in winter and super pony-trekking mecca in other seasons. This former British hill station vies with **Palagham** for fishing, trekking and hiking.

Out of Srinagar, one can also river and lake trek by shikara or, for larger groups, the donga. This is the big, flat-bottomed boat on which you will see families living almost Amsterdam barge-style along the River Jhelem in Srinagar.

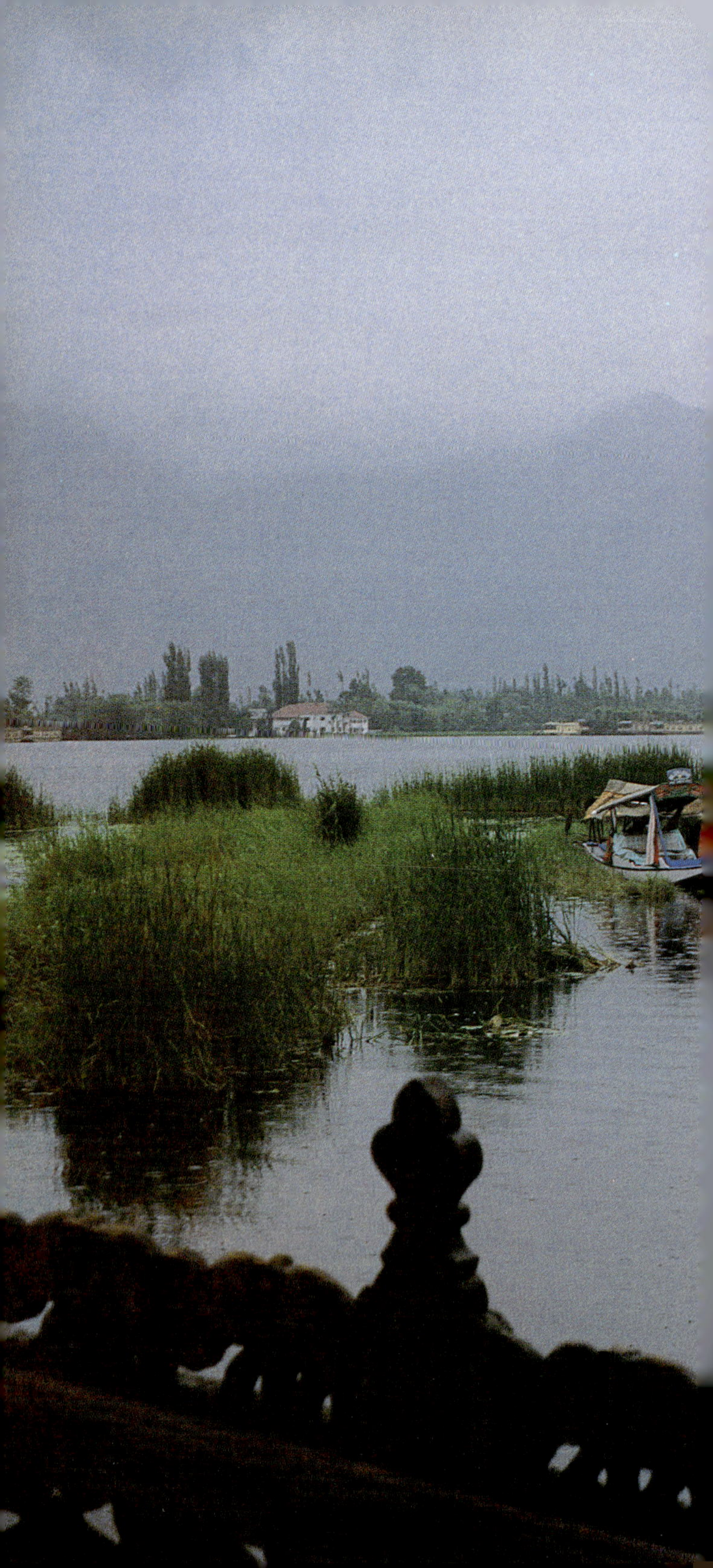

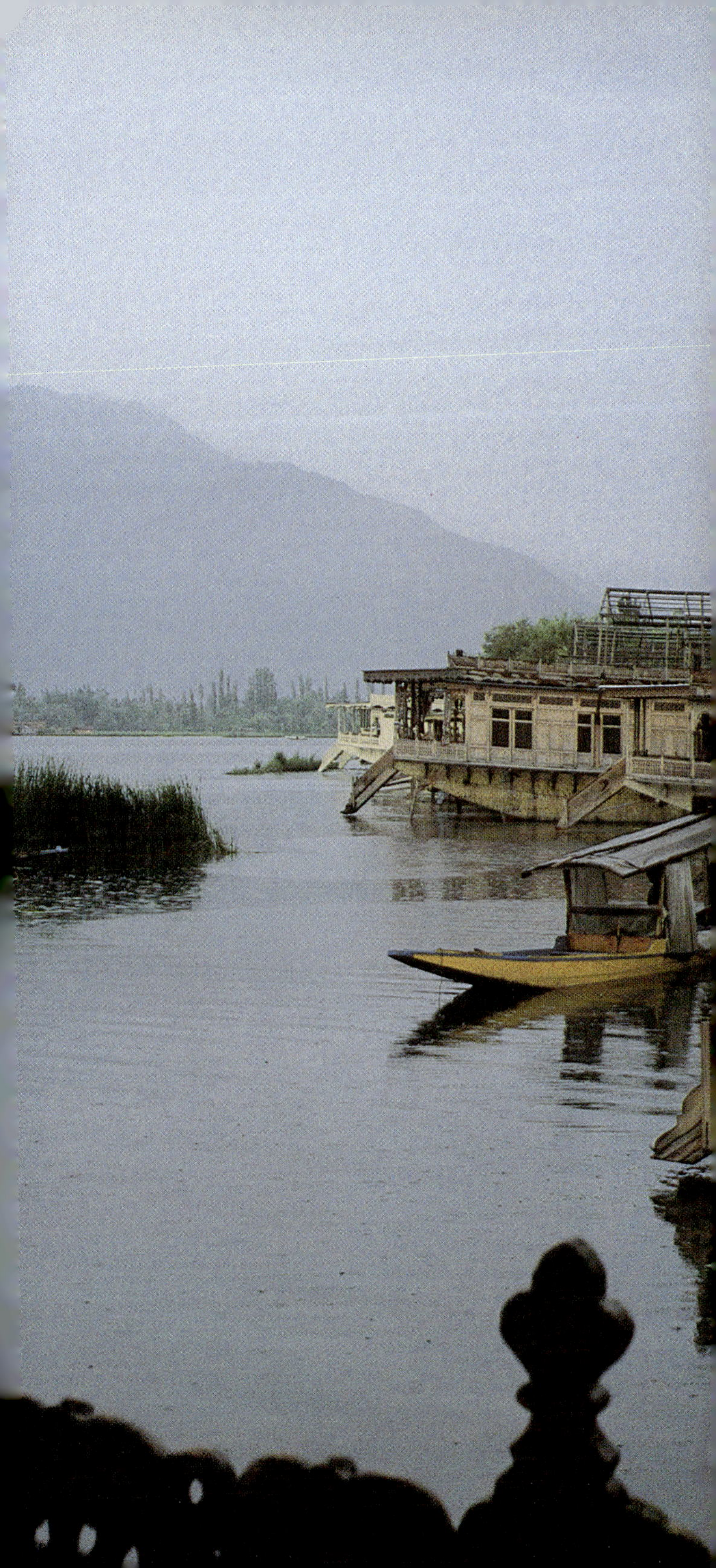

AGRA

The Taj and Fatehpursikri

From Delhi, a day trip by car, coach or train to the city of the fabled Taj Mahal, Agra, can be extended to a two or several day experience if your time allows. Agra is a half hour flight from Delhi. The road distance is 204 km.

First mentioned in history in the epic **Mahabharata**, Agra, now in the **State of Uttar Pradesh**, was also referred to in the 2nd century as Agara. Brought to prominence by **Akbar The Great**, the city was briefly the capital of the Moghul Empire.

The Red Fort

Akbar built the imposing Red Fort by the **River Yamuna** in 1565. It certainly rivals the fort of the same name in Old Delhi for attractions not only in red sandstone but marble. On the banks of the River Yamuna, it has several palaces and the stunning **Pearl Mosque**. Open from sunrise to sunset daily, it also has a sound and light display for which entrance, as to the fort by day, is charged.

Agra

The Taj Mahal

Later, in 1652 Emperor **Shah Jahan** constructed in white marble the tomb for his queen, **Mumtaz**. Bearing his 14th child, she died and, struck with grief, the emperor brought 20,000 workers to erect the monument to her memory. Regarded by many as the world's most wonderful monument which, in the heat, seems to float towards the heavens and is reflected in the geometric pools before it, the Taj Mahal includes 22 small domes, testimony to the number of years of its construction. Its major dome, almost 25 metres in height, is directly above **Mumtaz Mahal's tomb**. The emperor's tomb is next to hers, having been erected there by Shah Jahan's meglomaniacal son, **Aurangzeb**, who imprisoned his father for the last 16 years of the Shah's life.

The fantastic inlay work of semi-precious stones into marble must be observed. The Taj Mahal is open from sunrise to 7.30 p.m. There is a fee for entry every day except Friday.

> **INFOTIP:** Other guides may recommend the magic of viewing the Taj by moonlight. Because of vandalism and looting after dark, this has not been possible for some time. Be content to view the marvellous marble monument in different noods of light until sunset.

Itmad-ud-Daulah's Tomb

This impressive mausoleum was the predecessor of the Taj Mahal, completed by **Empress Nur Jehan** in 1628 in honour of her father. Smaller than the Taj, it is white marble on red sandstone with semi-precious stones inlaid in marble in the most intricate of designs.

Fatehpursikri

About 37 km west of Agra is the former capital which was moved from Agra by Akba after a holyman Christi, who lived in the village, prophesized the emperor, then without heir, would have a son. The child, named **Salim**, later became known as **Jehangir**.

The splendid redstone city built by Akbar in gratitude was beyond imagination in riches and also included buildings in which many religions were worshipped in the hope of amalgamation. By contrast, Akbar still maintained a building - **Ankh Michauli** - meaning blind man's buff, in which he played this game with the women of his vast harem. His women were also used as pieces in a giant chess board.

Agra

The fascinating complex includes **Jami Masjid**, an impressive, elaborate mosque for 10,000 people entered via India's tallest gateway of 54 metres. Behind it is Christi's tomb to which thousands of childless Hindu and Muslim women make pilgrimage yearly.

The fort, with its palaces and mosques, secular and religious buildings, declined due to of lack of water supply but remains well preserved though deserted apart from tourists and pilgrims. It is well worth the deviation from Agra.

Agra has a variety of accommodations and guided tours (embracing in a day, the Taj Mahal, Red Fort and Fatepurskiri.)

> **INFOTIP:** Buy such a tour ticket on the Taj Express after you leave Delhi or book an ITDC coach tour in Delhi.

You can do it yourself with tourist taxi or rickshaw on a daily basis. As Agra is sprawling, it's hard to walk if time is short.

Taj Mahal, Agra

Agra

For reputable transport, contact the GITO, 191, The Mall. Tel: 72377, which also has plenty of literature. Tours and guides can also be organized here.

> **INFOTIP:** Be wary of drivers and unlicensed guides who will want to drop you for a moment into a nice cool shop-complex for a refreshing drink and a browse. As India's most tourized centre, Agra is full of people out for their cut, their commission out of what you buy. If you just wish to sightsee, be very firm.

Then again, the inlaid marble work of Agra's marvellous monuments is attractive and here, you may wish to buy examples in tables, boxes etc. Check it's not scratchable alabaster. Also look for leather, brasswear, saris, carpets and fine jewellery.

Agra has super north Indian cuisine, particularly if you're into vegetarian. A good place for this (meat dishes too) is the Hotel Ashok. For top thali and Muglai, try the Mughal Sheraton.

Agra

The Palace on Wheels

Although our Infoguides are mindful of visitors who wish to spend maximum time in the city of destination, in this case Delhi, with perhaps two to three days sidetripping to places such as Srinagar and Agra, we do recommend to those who have seven days disposal out of Delhi a journey that will clacketty-clack one through seven cities by rail in the manner of the **Maharajahs** and the **Viceroys** of the **Raj**. This is by the **Palace on Wheels** with a little help from an elephant and camel or two, plus a laid-back boatman or several.

Opulent carriages built from 1898 to 1937 with antique fittings, two restaurant cars, and an observation, library and bar carriage are steam-driven by night and the sightseeing is done by day. The bathrooms are modern.

Cities visited are **Jaipur**, the pink city, with its **City Palace, Jantar Mantar, State Emporium, Amber Fort** (including elephant ride,) and **Nahargarh Fort** and then **Chittaurgarh** and **Udaipur** where two lake trips across its shimmering lakes are scheduled. Then come the the desert kingdom of **Jaisalmer** (camel rides here) and **Jodhpur**, of the marble cenotaphs, with their sights, including forts, and **Bharatpur** with its bird sanctuary. The Agra stop includes first **Fotehpursikri** then the Red Fort and the crowning glory, the **Taj Mahal**.

Breakfast is always on board and some other meals, whether on the train or in an exciting city at five star and-or palace hotels, are accompanied by cultural performances reflecting the rhythm of the State of Rajasthan.

Kashmir Houses along the canal

Agra

GURU GOVIND SINGH MARG
Dayabasti
NORTHERN RAILWAY
(NAJAFGARH ROAD)
SHIVAJI MARG
PATEL ROAD
Ayurvedic Hospital
NARAINA ROAD
SADHU VASWANI MARG (PUSA ROAD)
SHANKAR ROAD
RING ROAD
NDMC Indoor Stadium & Pool
RIDGE ROAD
UPPER LINK ROAD
WILLINGDON
NICHOLSON RANGES
STATION ROAD
SADAR PATEL MARG
PANCHSHEEL
Maurya Sheraton
Moti Bagh
PATH
PARADE ROAD
Harbaksh Stadium
SHANTI PATH
RAO TULARAM ROAD
PALAM
VIVEKANAND MARG
Jawaharlal Nehru Univeristy Campus
Temple
Mosque
Church
Post Office
Police Station
Hotel
Park
Important Building
0
0.5
1
KILOMETRES

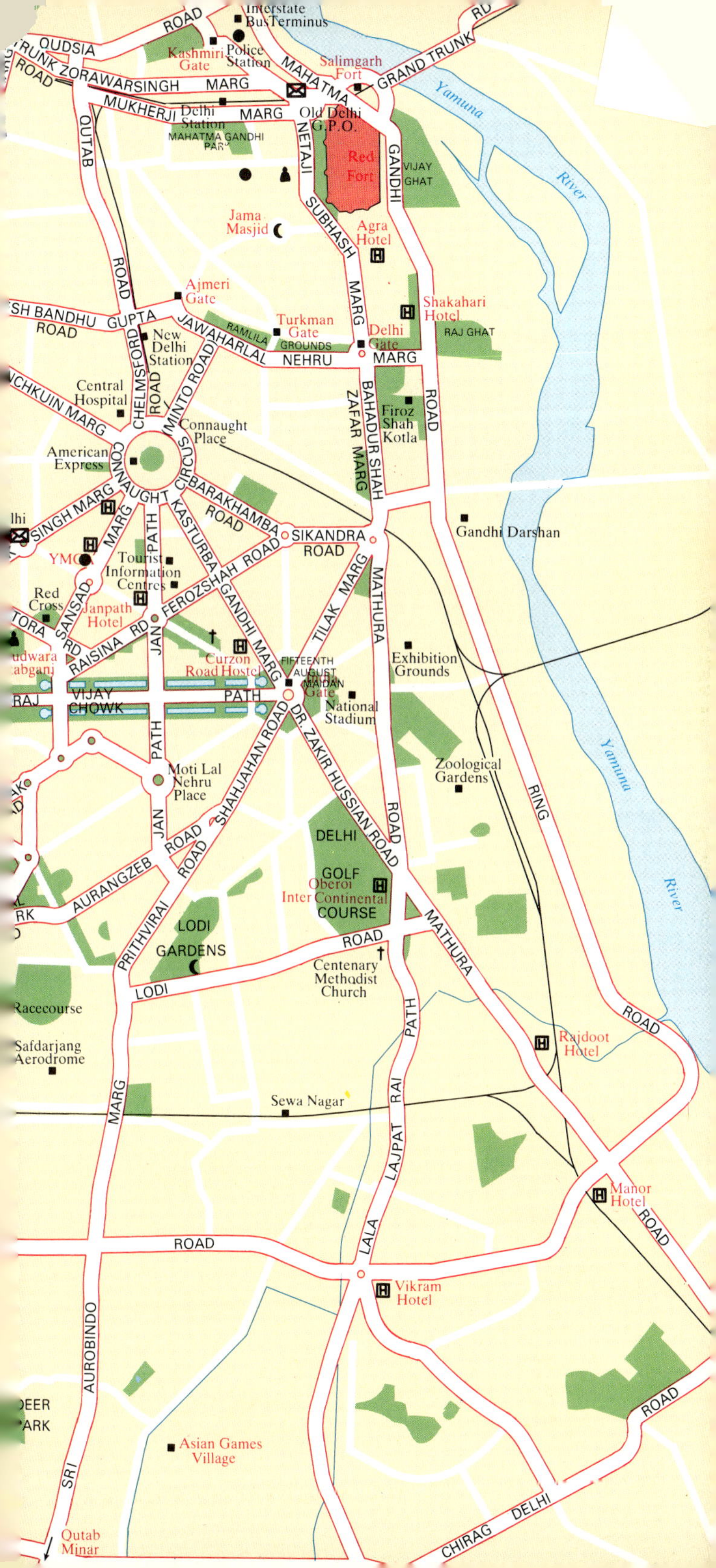
Interstate BusTerminus
Kashmiri Gate
Police Station
Salimgarh Fort
QUDSIA
ROAD
TRUNK ROAD
ZORAWARSINGH MARG
MAHATMA
GRAND TRUNK
RD
MUKHERJI MARG
Delhi Station
MAHATMA GANDHI PARK
Old Delhi G.P.O.
Red Fort
NETAJI SUBHASH MARG
GANDHI
VIJAY GHAT
Yamuna
River
QUTAB ROAD
Jama Masjid
Agra Hotel
Ajmeri Gate
Shakahari Hotel
Turkman Gate
Delhi Gate
RAMLILA GROUNDS
RAJ GHAT
SH BANDHU GUPTA ROAD
New Delhi Station
CHELMSFORD ROAD
JAWAHARLAL NEHRU MARG
MINTO ROAD
Central Hospital
NCHKUIN MARG
Connaught Place
BAHADUR SHAH ZAFAR MARG
Firoz Shah Kotla
ROAD
American Express
CONNAUGHT CIRCUS
BARAKHAMBA ROAD
lhi
SINGH MARG
MARG
PATH
KASTURBA GANDHI MARG
SIKANDRA ROAD
Gandhi Darshan
YMCA
Tourist Information Centres
FEROZSHAH ROAD
TILAK MARG
MATHURA
Red Cross
SANSAD
Janpath Hotel
TORA RD
RAISINA RD
JAN
Curzon Road Hotel
FIFTEENTH AUGUST MAIDAN
India Gate
Exhibition Grounds
udwara abganj
RAJ
VIJAY CHOWK
PATH
National Stadium
DR. ZAKIR HUSSIAN ROAD
SHAHJAHAN ROAD
Zoological Gardens
Moti Lal Nehru Place
JAN PATH
ROAD
RING
Yamuna
River
DELHI GOLF COURSE
Oberoi Inter Continental
AURANGZEB ROAD
RK
PRITHVIRAI ROAD
LODI GARDENS
ROAD
MATHURA
Centenary Methodist Church
LODI
Racecourse
Safdarjang Aerodrome
PATH
RAI
ROAD
Rajdoot Hotel
MARG
Sewa Nagar
LAJPAT
Manor Hotel
ROAD
ROAD
LALA
Vikram Hotel
AUROBINDO
DEER PARK
Asian Games Village
ROAD
SRI
DELHI
CHIRAG
Qutab Minar

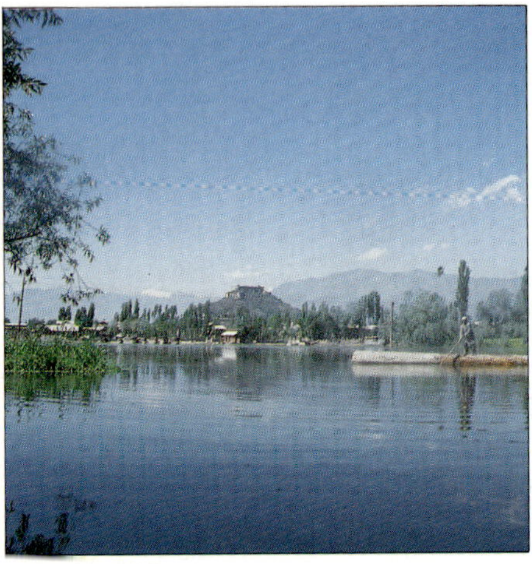

PART III
Accommodation

Jantar Mantar

HOTELS

GENERAL NOTES

The third section of this Info-Guide is an up-to-date list of hotels in Delhi, its suburbs and Srinagar in descending order of excellence from five star deluxe, through five, four, three, two to one star.

The criteria for classification has been set by India's Department of Tourism and is based on all facilities of each, individual establishment from the size of the room to the qualifications of hotel personnel. Most of the hotels listed have been government approved. Gaining star-rating is a long and involved process in India, involving many inspections and time in which the hotels must fulfill the standards required to meet the star-rating sought.

Star-ratings do not indicate that all prices in one category are the same. They can vary. Also each vary in the type of additional taxes charges. The taxes can include government, sales, luxury, service and taxes on food and liquor. Where there is a service charge, tipping is not expected. Business travellers will also see at a glance the facilities available.

If air conditioning is available, it will be listed.

Some hotels have listed under their facilities Bar Permit or Permit Room. This means that to be able to order alcohol other than beer, visitors must produce their permit to do so in areas where there is partial prohibition. See the Restaurant/ Food section of this book for details on gaining the permit.

When they are good, Indian hotels are very very good, superior in the world. In most accommodations, accounts must be paid in foreign currency - cash, travellers' cheques or by credit card. Inquire about the method of payment expected in hotels which do not list credit card facilities when booking or checking in.

Special rates are usually applicable in the monsoon season and/or for groups.

The Indian Tourist Development Corporation operates a chain of hotels under the name Ashok. From two to five star, these are inevitably reliable. Inquire of the Government of India Tourist Office in your home country about special discount rates applicable if your Indian sojourn will be in **Ashok** hotels, with the exception of Srinagar, where as yet, there is no Ashok hotel.

Checkout times vary from 10 a.m. to noon. Some hotels, if not fully pre-booked, will offer special day room rates to late- departing travellers.

Accommodation

When booking, inquire on which plan the room rate is structured. The American Plan includes room and three meals. Modified American Plan is room, breakfast, lunch or dinner. The European Plan is room only.

Where car rental is listed as a facility, this is rental with driver.

CAMPING

There are two tourist camping parks in Delhi, the first opposite the J.P. arayan Hospital, **Jawaharlal Nehru Marg**, Tel: 278929, the second at **Qudsia Gardens**, opposite the Interstate Bus Terminus, Tel: 2523121.

Legend

R - Restaurants/Dining Room
C - Conference Rooms
B - Bars
SP - Swimming Pool
TV - Television/Video
RM - Room Service
T - Tennis Court
G - Golf Course
AC - Air Conditioned
SS - Secretarial Services
D - Discotheque
CC - Credit Cards
CR - Car Rental
BP - Bar Permit

DELHI

ASHOK HOTEL
Chankyapuri
New Delhi 110 021
Tel. 60 0121, 60 0412
R, C, B, SP, TV, RM, T, G, AC

HYATT REGENCY DELHI
Bhikaiji Cama Place
Ring Road
New Delhi 110 066
Tel. 60 9911
AC, R, C, B, SP, TV, RM, T, G

THE OBEROI
Dr. Zakir Hussain Marg
New Delhi 110 003
Tel. 36 3030
AC, RM, SS, C, TV, SP

THE TAJ MAHAL HOTEL
No 1 Mansingh Road
New Delhi 110 011
Tel. 301 6162
Fax. (011) 301 7299
AC, C, R, B, TV, D, SP, SS

Accommodation

TAJ PALACE INTERCONT
2 Sardar Patel Marg
Diplomatic Enclave
New Delhi 110 021
Tel. 301 0404
Fax. (011) 301 1252
AC, SP, SS, C, R, B, TV

CENTAUR HOTEL
I.G.I. Airport
New Delhi 110 037
Tel. 545 2223, 548 1411
AC, R, C, B, SS, SP, T

CLARIDGES HOTEL
12 Aurangzeb Road
New Delhi 110 011
Tel. 301 0211
R, AC, C, SP, SS, TV

CENTRAL COURT HOTEL
Connaught Circus
New Delhi 110 001
Tel. 331 5013
R, AC

WELCOMGROUP MAURYA SHERATON
Diplomatic Enclave
New Delhi 110 021
Tel. 301 0101
AC, C, B, R, SP, TV, SS, T

THE CONNAUGHT PALACE
37 Shaheed Bhagat Singh Marg
New Delhi 110 001
Tel. 34 4225
R, AC, TV, RM, SS, B, C

HOTEL KANISHKA
19 Ashok Road
New Delhi 110 001
Tel. 332 4422
R, AC, C, B, SP, TV, RM, D

LE MERIDIEN
Windsor Place
Janpath
New Delhi 110 011
Tel. 38 3960
R, AC, SP, SS, C

Oberoi lobby

Accommodation

Kerry Kenihan, on Golden Lotus

HOTEL IMPERIAL
Janpath
New Delhi 110 001
Tel. 332 5332
R, AC, SP, TV, C

QUTAB HOTEL
Off Sri Aurobindo Marg
New Delhi 110 016
Tel. 66 0060
R, AC, C, B, SP, TV, RM, T

HOTEL SIDDHARTH
3 Rajendra Place
New Delhi 110 008
Tel. 571 2501
R, AC, RM, SS

HOTEL AMBASSADOR
Sujan Singh Park
New Delhi 110 003
Tel. 69 0391
R, AC, RM, B, C, D

PARK HOTEL
15 Parliament Street
New Delhi 110 001
Tel. 35 2477
R, AC, SP, C, SS, TV

HOTEL SAMRAT
Chanakyapuri
New Delhi 110 021
Tel. 60 3030
R, AC, C, B, SP, TV

HOTEL SOFITEL SURYA
Friends Colony
New Delhi 110 065
Tel. 683 5070
R, AC, SP, C, SS

HOTEL VASANT CONT
Vasant Vihar
New Delhi 110 057
Tel. 67 8800
R, AC, TV, SS, SP, RM

Accommodation

HOTEL DIPLOMAT
9 Sardar Patel Road
New Delhi 110 021
Tel. 301 0204
R, AC, B, RM, TV

HOTEL HANS PLAZA
15 Barakhamba Road
New Dehli 110 001
Tel. 331 6868
R, AC

HOTEL JANPATH
Janpath
New Delhi 110 001
Tel. 332 0070
R, AC, C, B, TV, RM

HOTEL MARINA
G-59 Connaught Circus
New Delhi
Tel. 332 4658
R, AC, C, TV, B, RM

OBEROI MAIDENS
7 Sham Nath Marg
Delhi 110 054
Tel. 252 5464
R, AC, SP, T, TV, RM

HOTEL RAJDOOT PVT LTD
Mathura Road
New Delhi 110 014
Tel. 69 9583-10
R, AC, B, SP, TV

HOTEL ALKA
16/90 Connaught Circus
New Delhi 110 001
Tel. 34 4328
R, AC

HOTEL BROADWAY
4/15A Asaf Ali Road
New Delhi 110 002
Tel. 27 3821
R, AC, C, B, TV

Accommodation

HOTEL SOBTI
2397/98 Hardian Singh Road
Karol Bagh
New Delhi 110 005
Tel. 572 9065
R, AC, TV, RM

HOTEL VIKRAM
Ring Road
Lajpat Nagar
New Delhi 110 024
Tel. 643 6451
R, AC, TV, RM, SP, B, C

YORK HOTEL
K-Block Connaught Circus
New Delhi 110 001
Tel. 332 3769, 332 3019
R, AC, TV, RM, B

HOTEL FLORA
Dayanand Road
Daryaganj
New Delhi 110 002
Tel. 27 3634-35-36
R, AC, C, TV, RM

NIRULA'S HOTEL
L Block Connaught Circus
New Delhi 110 001
Tel. 332 2419
R, AC, B, C, TV

HOTEL PRESIDENT
4/23-B Asaf Ali Road
New Delhi 110 002
Tel. 27 7836-38
R, AC, TV, B

HOTEL RANJIT
Maharaja Ranjit Singh Road
New Delhi 110 002
Tel. 331 1256
R, AC, C, B, SP, TV

SARTAJ HOTEL
A-3 Green Park
New Delhi 110 016
Tel. 66 7759, 66 3277
R, AC, C, B, TV, SS

HOST INN
F-33 Connaught Place
New Delhi 110 001
Tel. 331 0431
R, AC, TV

HOTEL NEERU PVT LTD
10 Netaji Subhash Marg
Darya Ganj
New Delhi 110 002
Tel. 27 8522, 27 8756
R, AC, B

HOTEL THE NEST
Corner House
11 Qutab Marg
New Delhi 110 055
Tel. 52 6614, 52 6429
AC, TV

HOTEL SHIELA
9 Qutab Road
Pawa House
New Delhi 110 055
Tel. 52 5603, 52 5478
R, AC, RM

TERA HOTEL
2802 Bara Bazar
Kashmere Gate
Delhi 110 006
R, C, TV

ASHOK YATRI NIWAS
19 Ashok Road
New Delhi 110 001
Tel. 332 4511
R, C, B

HOTEL ASIAN INTERNATIONAL
Janpath lane
New Delhi 110 001
Tel. 332 1636
R, AC

HOTEL FIFTY FIVE
H-55 Connaught Circus
New Delhi 110 001
Tel. 332 1244, 332 1278
R, AC, RM, B, TV

Accommodation

LODHI HOTEL
Lala Lajpat Rai Marg
New Delhi 110 003
Tel. 36 2422
R, AC, C, B, SP, RM, TV

MANOR HOTEL
77 Friends Colony West
New Delhi 110 065
Tel. 63 2171, 63 2511
R, AC, C, SP, T

HOTEL METRO
N-49 Connaught Circus
Janpath
New Delhi 110 001
Tel. 331 3856, 331 3805
AC, CC

HOTEL REGAL
S.P. Mukerjee Marg
Delhi 110 006
Tel. 252 6197
R, AC, TV

NEW DELHI YMCA
Jai Singh Road
New Delhi 110 001
Tel. 31 1915, 31 1847
R, AC, C, T, SP

HOTEL BHAGIRATH PALACE
Opposite Red Fort
Chandni Chowk
Delhi 110 006
Tel. 23 6223
R, B, TV, AC

Accommodation

SRINAGAR

HOTEL BROADWAY
Maulana Azad Road
Srinagar
Tel. 79101-2, 79201-2
R, AC, TV, RM, B, SP, C, SS

THE OBEROI PALACE
Gupkar Road
Srinagar
Tel. 75751-2-3, 75651
R, C, TV, SS

HOTEL PAMPOSH
Residency Road
Srinagar
Tel. 75601-2
R, C, TV

HOTEL ZARARVAN
The Boulevard
Srinagar 190 001
Tel. 71441-42
R, AC, C, TV, RM

HOTEL BOULEVARD
Srinagar 190 001
Tel. 77089, 77153

HOTEL ORNATE NEHRUS
Boulevard
Srinagar 190 001
Tel. 73641
R, C, TV

CENTAUR LAKE VIEW HOTEL
Chasmeshahi
Sringar (J&K) 190 001
Tel. 75667, 71215
R, AC, SS, SP, T

HOTEL TRAMBOO CONT
Boulevard
Dal Lake
Srinagar 190 001
Tel. 73914, 71718
R, TV, RM

ASIA BROWN PALACE
Boulevard
Srinagar Kashmir
Tel. 73903, 73856
R

HOTEL GULMARG
Boulevard
Srinagar Kashmir
Tel. 71331-35
R, AC, TV, RM

HOTEL JEHANGIR
Jehangir Chowk
Budshah Bridge
Srinagar 190 001 (J&K)
Tel. 71830, 71831
R, TV

HOTEL MAZDA
Boulevard Road
Srinagar
Tel. 72842, 75534

MEENA BAZAAR
Group of Houseboats
Srinagar 190 001
Tel. 74044 & 77662
R

METRO HOTEL
Dalgate
Srinagar 190 001
Tel. 77126, 78256
R, TV

HOTEL NEW SHALIMAR
Boulevard Road
Dal Lake
Srinagar 190 001
Tel. 74427, 73339

WELCOMGROUP GURKHA
Houseboats
Srinagar 190 001
Tel. 75229, 73848

Himalayan Foothills

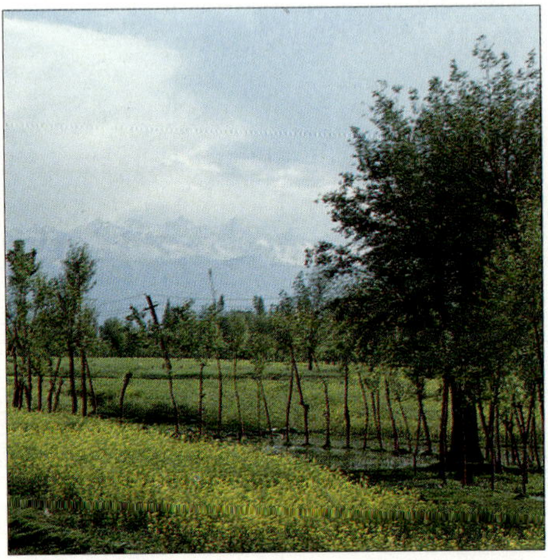

PART IV
Practical Information

PRACTICAL INFORMATION

A-Z Summary

ADVANCE PLANNING	117
CRIME	142
CURRENCY	122
ELECTRICITY	123
EMERGENCIES	140
ENTERTAINMENT	124
Art Galleries and Museums	124
Childrens Entertainment	124
Cinemas	125
ENTRY REGULATIONS	120
Customs	120
Duty Free Imports	120
EXHIBITIONS	126
FESTIVALS	126
Festivals in Kashmir	130
GETTING AROUND DELHI	131
GETTING AROUND OUTSIDE DELHI	132
GETTING TO INDIA	122
HELP	138
Consulates/Embassies	138
LIBRARIES WITH BOOKS IN ENGLISH	143
MOTORING	143
POST OFFICE	144
PUBLICATIONS IN ENGLISH	144
RADIO/TELEVISION	130
RELIGIOUS SERVICES IN ENGLISH	145
RESTAURANTS REGIONAL & INTERNATIONAL	155-160
RESTAURANTS & NIGHTLIFE	146
SEMINARS	130
SHOPPING	160
SPORTS AND ATHLETICS	164
Sports in Kashmir	167
TELEPHONE AND TELEGRAPH	168
THEATRE AND MUSIC	126
TIME	170
TIPPING	170
TOURIST SERVICES	171
TOURS	174
TRAVEL AGENTS & PRIVATE OPERATORS	175

Along the Canals

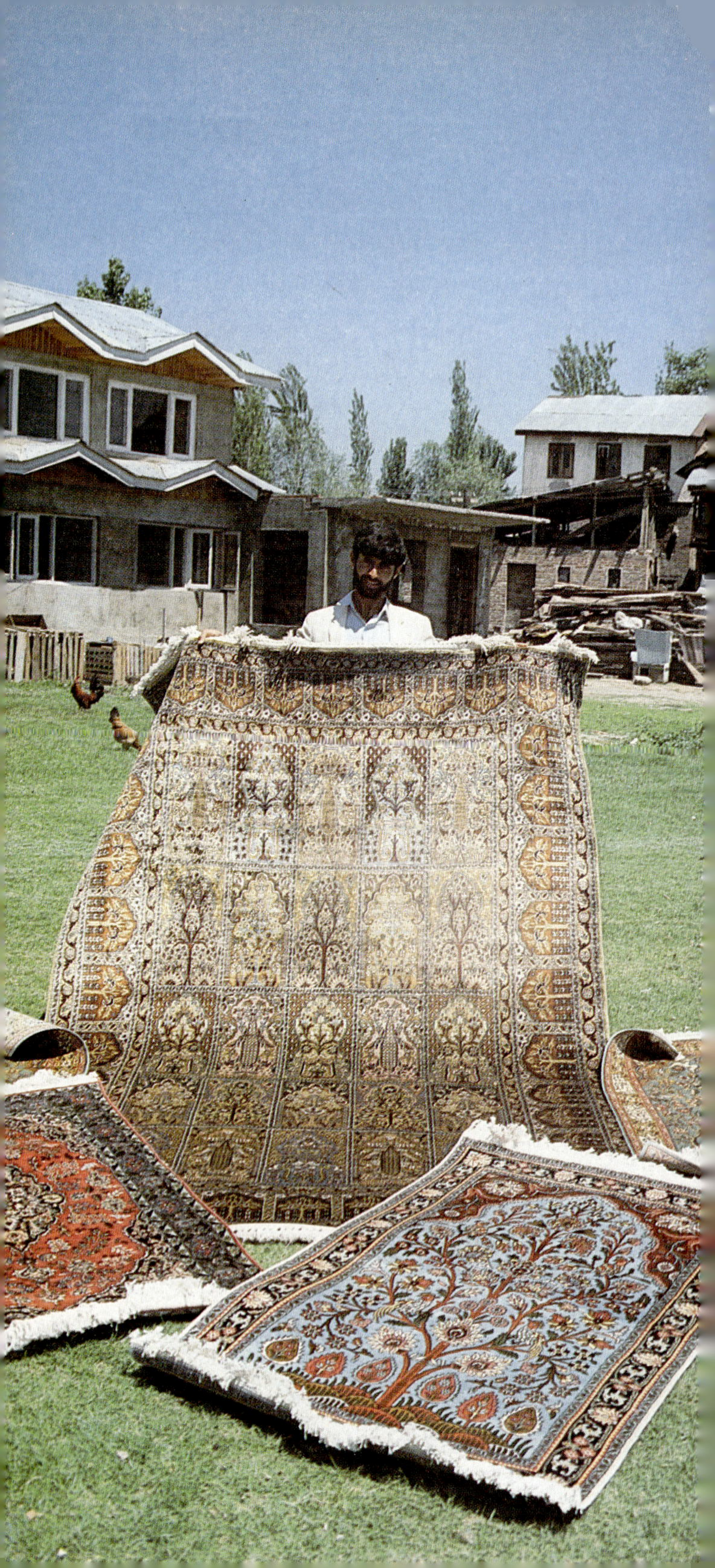

ADVANCE PLANNING

The Government of India Tourist Office, the Tourist Development Corporation and Air India has offices in many parts of the world to help you plan your itinerary or stopover. See page .

What to bring

Documents:
All visitors to India need a current passport and visa. Three types of visa are issued - tourist, non-tourist and entry. It depends on the purpose of the visit. Tourist visas for 90 days may be extended by applying to Foreigners Regional Registration offices in Bombay, Delhi, Madras or Calcutta or at district headquarters of Superintendent of Police. In Delhi, the Foreigners Regional Registration Office is on the first floor, Hans Bhawan, Tilak Bridge. Tel: 3318179.

People in transit to other parts of the world must produce onward tickets in order to gain a transit visa of 15 days to be used within three months of the issuing date. A double-way transit visa allows the visitor two trips through India for a maximum of 15 days each time.

First issued for 90 days to people intending professional or business dealings in India, an entry visa can be extended for a further 90 days. If a trip could exceed extensions of six months, application must be made two months in advance to an Indian Embassy or Mission out of India.

Visa issuing fees are charged by embassies abroad to foreigners with the exception of nationals from Afghanistan, Czechoslovakia, Denmark, Greece, Hungary, Iran, Norway, Poland, Rumania, Russia, San Marino, Sweden, Uruguay and Yugoslavia.

Also bring credit cards and a driver's licence, preferably an international licence which may be needed for motor cycle rental only if you happen to travel on to Goa in West India, just about the only place a foreign visitor can rent in India.

Americans will need receipts of purchases for their own customs. All foreigners should check with their own customs departments on current legislation on the importation home of ivory.

Clothing:
India is so vast that its climatic conditions vary greatly but for Delhi bring the lightest of cotton garments between February and May when temperatures are likely to reach

Practical Information

the high 40s. At the same time in Kashmir, temperatures are around the pleasant 20s and evenings can be cooler so bring a wool wrap or pullover. In winter, pack woollens for Delhi and extra warm clothing for Kashmir which usually is snow-clad. You can buy suitable clothing very cheaply in India.

The Indian people dress modestly so bear this in mind when dressing for the street and excursions which may include places of religious worship. Brief shorts and tops will offend. Men can wear shorts but women should not. Men should not go bare chested. Some top class hotels may require neat, casual dress in restaurants.

Pack a swimming costume. Nude and topless bathing is not permitted in Delhi pools or Srinagar's lakes in Kashmir.

Odds and Ends:

A towel for swimming. Top hotels with pools provide them to guests (some free, others for a small fee,) but more modest establishments do not. Also bring a face towel to remain moist in a plastic bag to refresh yourself if driving in non- airconditioned vehicles. Pack a portable clothes line, health (see below) and personal necessities such as spectacles, contact lenses and sun cream. Women should bring their preferred brands of cosmetics, toiletries and tampons as they may be unavailable. Bring tissues to act as toilet paper in emergencies. Padlock your suitcase and bring another with you for your door if you are staying in accommodations which may have inadequate security.

Toilet paper and soap are not provided in trains. Bring your own.

While films and camera batteries are available in the cities and larger towns, don't run the risk of running out and bring extra.

> **INFOTIP:** Passengers flying in on Air India and flying internally are not permitted to include some types of batteries, such as those powering certain cameras, in their hand luggage. Pack them (and maybe the appliance well- wrapped in clothing) in luggage to be stowed in the cargo hold as buying batteries at your destination will represent inconvenience and may not be immediately available.

Medical Tips:

Take out adequate health cover in your travel insurance. Should you become ill, you will need it against private hospital care or the attentions of a hotel's doctor whose charges may be high. Naturally, keep all receipts for fees

Practical Information

charged to present on your return. If you intend arriving via a yellow fever infected country, ensure you are vaccinated before leaving home. This is India's only vaccination requirement.

However, because you may travel in areas where sanitation is poor, it is strongly recommended that you consult your doctor before leaving and consider having cholera, combined tetanus/typhoid, and gamma globulin (against hepatitus A,) innoculations. If you are a frequent traveller to eastern countries, also consider protection against hepatitus B.

If you are travelling in both northern and southern India, tell your doctor. Two different tablets to protect you against two strains of malaria will be prescribed. Chloroquine should not be taken by pregnant women. While anti-malarial preparations are available cheaply in India, courses should be begun before arrival. Seek a home consultation as soon as your plans are known to give yourself plenty of time for vaccinations to become effective.

Rabies has not been eradicated in India and it is fatal. Keep away from all animals, including cute monkeys. If you are bitten by any creature, clean the wound well and go to a city hospital for injections. Private, Christian hospitals have the highest standards.

Practical Information

Take note of the generic names of any prescription drugs to show to a pharmacist in case you run out or lose them. Most 5-star hotels have drugstores but preparations may be under different brand names. If you are not staying at a 5-star, head for one if you need assistance. English will be spoken.

Ask your doctor to prescribe medications against most unfortunate contigencies. Your kit should include preparations for diarrhoea, constipation, nausea and vomiting and a broad spectrum antibiotic against the type of infections you could pick up at home. Include analgesics, anti-malarials, which you'll continue to take during your visit, insect repellent (mosquito deterrent,) bandaids and anticeptic cream.

Do not bring narcotic drugs to India and refuse any offers of **ganja** for sale. You may be approached, particularly if young and not staying in the better hotels.

Despite tales of Delhi belly, you can enjoy India without being ill if you take adequate precautions. If you are unaccustomed to spicy food, introduce it to your system gradually. NEVER drink water that is not bottled mineral water or which has not been solidly boiled. Some big hotels have purified water on tap. Others may offer water that has been filtered but not boiled. Ask. If in doubt, ask for boiling water with which to make tea and let it cool or boil your own water with an immersion heater.

Entry Regulations

See above under Documents

Customs

At Delhi's Indira Gandhi international airport, there is a red, something-to-declare lane and a green 'nothing to declare' lane. On arrival, your declaration may be verbal or you may be required to give up a form stating your agreement to re-export valuables such as jewellery, cameras etc. You may be required to present all your baggage to be x-rayed before you LEAVE Delhi airport so that what you are importing can be determined - but neither situation always applies.

Duty Free Imports

Visitors to India for from between 24 hours and six months, provided not more than six visits are made in one year, can import personal belongings, including clothing, jewellery, one camera, one video-camera. one musical instrument, one radio, one tape recorder, a portable typewriter and sports equipment. Travel souvenirs must not exceed the value of 500 rupees duty free, regardless of the type of visa issued. Visitors of Indian origin can import these goods to the value of 1,000 rupees. (The extra is allowed for gifts to families.) A firearm may be imported provided a possession licence gained in advance or proof of exemption is produced.

Importation of pets is permitted with a combined health and rabies exemption certificate from a qualified veterinarian issued no more than a week before arrival.

Cigarettes: 200 or 50 cigars or 250 grammes of tobacco.
Alcohol: 1 bottle (.95 litre.)
Perfume: 2 oz.
Cologne: one quarter litre.

Goods in excess of the maximum permitted are subject to 325 per cent import duty unless the re-exportation guarantee has been signed. Visitors under age 17 may import one quarter of the adult allowance.

Trekker's and Skiiers Paradise

Practical Information

Currency

Unlimited currency may be imported provided an excess of US1000 is declared. Import and export of Indian rupees is prohibited. Money should be changed only at recognized banks and official money changers and receipted. Insist on a receipt if it is not given as it is necessary to produce this evidence in order to re- exchange rupees for foreign currency on leaving India.

Foreign travellers, including those of Indian origin, must pay major expenses including hotel accounts, airline fares and special train tickets in foreign currency or by foreign credit card. The rupee is the Indian unit, comprised of 100 paise.

GETTING TO INDIA

By Air:

India is connected by air from all parts of the world. Flights may be through or via transfer connections to connecting airports. There are also many air charters

By Rail:

In the past, it has been possible to enter India from Pakistan with lots of hassles but check with the Government of India Tourist Office on political relationships between the two countries in advance.

By Road:

The traditional land route from Europe via France, Germany, Yugoslavia, Bulgaria, Turkey, Iran and Pakistan has for some years been inadvisable for private motorists because of political turmoil in countries adjacent to this route. A few overland bus tours are still operated intermittently from London and inquiries should be made with GITO or major travel agents such as Thomas Cook and American Express. The automobile associations of western countries should be approached by any private motorists to obtain current information on the advisability of attempting the journey alone.

By Sea:

India is no longer connected by regular passenger ship services to western countries but several cruise lines include major Indian ports on some of their round-the-world itineraries. Inquiries should be made of major travel agents. However, some freighter lines which do call at

Practical Information

major Indian ports such as Bombay, Calcutta and Madras offer limited passenger accommodation. These lines include the British India Steam Navigation Company and the American President Lines. Private yachtsmen need valid ship's documents.

> **INFOTIP:** As the Indrail Pass is issued on the basis of the class of travel, i.e. First Class Air Conditioned, it might be wise to ascertain if the trains you intent to use do in fact have air conditioned First Class carriages. If not, save and buy a normal First Class pass.

Store by the Lake

Electricity

The electric current in India is 220/250 volts and 50 cycles. It is AC almost everywhere.

Practical Information

Entertainment

Art Galleries and Museums

Delhi has several major museums and art galleries.
Delhi Shilpi Chakra, 19 Shankar Market.
Dhoominal Art Gallery, 8A Connaught Place.
Tel: 310839.
Fine Arts Gallery, Rafi Marg.Tel: 381315.
Gallery Chanakya, 114 Yashwant Place,
Chanakyapuri.Tel: 672556.
Gallery Lalit Kala Academy, Rabindra Bhawan, Ferozeshah Rd. Tel: 387 241.
National Gallery of Modern Art, Jaipur House, Dr. Zakir Hussain Marg. Tel: 382835. Closed Monday.
Sridharani Art Gallery, 205, Tansen Marg.Tel: 388833.
Yavanika Sangeet Natak Academy, Rabindra Bhawan, Ferozeshah Rd. Tel: 387246.
Air Force Museum, Palam Marg. (Closed Tuesday.)
Bal Bhawan & National Children's Museum, 1, Kotla Rd. Tel: 3314701. (Closed Thursday.)
Crafts Museum, Prahati Maidan Exhibition Ground, Lal Bahadur Shastri Marg. Tel: 8040304.
International Dolls Museum, Nehru House, Bahadur Shah Zafar Marg. Tel: 3316974. (Closed Monday.)
Gandhi Smarak Sangrahalya, Opposite Raj Ghat.
Tel: 274746.(Closed Monday.)
National Museum, Janpath. Tel: 385441. Closed Monday.
National Museum of Natural History, FICCI Building, Barakhamba Rd. Tel: 384932. (Closed Monday.)
National Philatelic, Daktar Bhavan, Sardar Patel Square, Sansad Marg.Tel: 380230. (Closed Sunday.)
Nehru Memorial Museum, Teen Murti Marg.
Tel: 3015333. (Closed Monday.)
Rail Transport Museum, Chanakyapuri. Tel: 611803. (Closed Monday.)
Red Fort Museum of Arms & Weapons, Red Fort.
Tel: 275569. (Closed Friday.)
Tibet House, Institutional Area, Lodi Rd. Tel: 611515. (Closed Sunday.)

Children's Entertainment

The **International Dolls Museum** and the **Rail Transport Museum** listed above will be of particular interest to children as will be the **planetarium** at the **Nehru Museum** and the **Jantar Mantar**, (observatory) Parliament Road.

Practical Information

Breakfast on Flic

There are a few parks situated around Delhi. Many of the attractions suitable for adults will also be of interest to children, particularly the Children's Park at India Gate and the zoo on Mathura Rd. Tel: 619825.(Closed Friday.)
Babysitting: Inquire from Housekeeping at your hotel.

Cinemas

Few film productions in India are in English, so it is wise to check English language newspaper advertisements for those which are in English or have English sub-titles.
Delhi's major cinemas are:
Archana, Greater Kailash I. Tel: 6414559.
The Chanakya, Yashwant Place, Chanakyapuri.
Tel: 674009.
Eros, Jangpura Extension. Tel: 615482.
Kamal Safdarjang Enclace. Tel: 664633.
Liberty, New Rohtak Rd. Tel: 562998.
Odeon, Connaught Place. Tel: 352167.
Plaza, Connaught Place. Tel: 335753.
Regal, Connaught Place. Tel: 312254.
Rivoli, Connaught Circus. Tel: 312227.
Sheila, D. B. Gupta Marg. Tel: 528299.

Practical Information

THEATRE AND MUSIC

Dance, Music and Drama

Dance, also cultural performances of traditional Indian music and drama are regularly held at the following theatres and auditoria.
Akshara Theatre, 8-B, Baba Kharak Singh Marg.
Tel: 321910.
Alliance Francaise, E 4, East of Kailash. Tel: 6417574.
India International Centre, 40 Max Mueller Marg.
Tel: 619431.
Kamani Auditorium, Copernicus Marg. Tel: 388084.
AIFACS Theatre, Rafi Marg. Tel: 381401.
Sri Ram Centre, College Rd. Tel: 384307.
Indian Council for Cultural Relations, Azad Bhavan, Indraprastha Estate. Tel: 3319309.
Gandhi Memorial Hall, Bahadur Shah Zafar Marg.
Tel: 3311049.
Mavalankah Hall, Rafi Marg. Tel: 385592.
Parsi Anjuman Hall, Bahadur Shah Zafar Marg.
Tel: 324831.
Sapru House, Barakhamba Rd. Tel: 3317240.
Triveni Chamber Theatre, 205 Tansen Marg. Tel: 388833.
Siri Auditorium, Siri Fort Rd. Tel: 667674.
American Centre, 24 Kasurba Gandhi Marg. Tel: 3316831.
Delhi Symphony Society, 5 Ashok Rd. Tel: 387502.
Delhi Music Society, 8, Nyaya Marg, Chanakyapuri.
Tel: 3015331.

Exhibitions

Exhibitions and trade fairs are frequently located in Bombay. For current information on what's on during your visit, contact tbe Federation of Indian Chambers of Commerce and Industry, Federation House, Tansen Marg. Tel: 3319251. See also, BUSINESS GUIDE. For cultural exhibitions, see ART GALLERIES AND MUSEUMS.

FESTIVALS

Delhi has a wide variety of festivals, each of which is celebrated in a distinctive way by religious groups or on special days of State or national occasion. Everyone joins in and visitors are welcome to participate.

Practical Information

Chandni Chowk, Old Delhi

Here is the annual calendar. Dates alter slightly from year to year, so check with GITO or your travel agent.

January: Lohri is the celebration of the climax of winter. Children go about singing and coillecting money for firewood with which to set into bonfires which are then lit.
Republic Day, January 26 is celebrated as a national festival throughout India. It marks the adoption of India's constitution and is one of De;hi's most spectacular events. The armed services parade as do floars and brilliantly festonned elephants and camels. The President of India takes the saulte. The Beating Retreat ceremony is held. The scenes at Raj Path, Vijay Chowk are not to be missed.
Delhi Rose Show. Roses are display and floral arranging competitions are held at Safdarjang's tomb.

February/March: The Delhi Flower Show is held annually at Purana Qila in February.
Mahashivratri or Shivrati is a solemn festival devoted to the worship of one of the Hindu trinity, Lord Shiva. The one-day event is celebrated by religious ceremonies continuing through the night and the singing of devotional songs. There are processions to temples where mantras are chanted and lingams are annointed.
Horse Show. This February annual event is held at the Delhi Racecourse or Delhi Cantonment.

Practical Information

March/April: Holi is a boisterous festival observed all over India. People throw coloured water and powder over each other to celebrate the advent of Spring.

Jamshedji Navroz is New Year's day for the Parsi community who adhere to the Falsi calendar and celebrate with feasting. Ramnavami is the birthday of the Hindu hero, Lord Rama, one of 10 incarnations of Lord Vishnu. There are celebrations in his honour.

Good Friday is observed by all Indian Christians.

Mahavir Jayanti is the birthday of the 24th and last Jain tirthankara.

April/May: Shivaji Jayanti is the birthday of Chatrapati Shivaji, the legendary king from Maharashtra. It is celebrated with functions in his honour all over Bombay.

Id-Ul-Fita (Ramzan Id) marks with feasting and rejoicing the end of Ramzan, the Muslim time of fasting.

Buddh Purnima is Buddha's birthday.

Urs takes place in April-May and September-October when prayers and qawalis (chorus singing) are conducted at Hazrat Nizamuddin Aulia's tomb.

July/August: Naag Panchami is when live cobra (naag) or their images, are worshipped. There are religious ceremonies and milk offerings made to live cobra.

Id-ul-Zuha (Bakr-Id) is the Muslim day observed to commemorate the prophet Ibrahim's sacrifice of his son in obedience to a command of God. Prayers are offered and alms given to the poor.

Independence Day is celebrated on August 15, the anniversary of India's freedom, won on this day in 1947.

Janamashtami, or Gokul Ashtami, is the birthday of Lord Krishna and fun to watch as energetic young men form human pyramids to release earthern pots filled with curds, suppposedly Lord Krishna's favourite sweets, which are strung high across the streets.

August/September: Ganesh Chaturthi is the birthday of the elephant-headed god, Ganesh. Big decorated images of the elephant god are worshipped.

September/October: Phool Waion ki Sair is the festival in which Muslims and Hindus carry palm fronds to be rejuvenated and blessed at the Muslim shrine and the temple of Mehrauli. There are also cultural performances at Jahaz Mahal.

Dussehra or Navratri is a 10-day time of great festival in which nine nights are spent in the worship of Devi, the mother goddess of the Hindus. Temporary shrines are built for public worship. The festival is based on the epic story

Practical Information

of Ramayana and signifies the triumph of good over evil. It culminates on the 10th and last day with in the burning of effigies of Ravana, who was the epitomy of evil, by Rama, the god-hero. Delhi is a marvellous city in which to experience Dussehra.

Gandhi Jayanti is Mahatma Gandhi's birthday on October 2 and is celebrated with reverence, throughout India.

October/November: Diwali is India's brightest festival. Each village, town and city becomes a fairyland of candles, lamps and millions of electric lights illuminating homes and public buildings. The goddess of wealth and prosperity, Laxmi, is worshipped and it is fitting that this signifies the New Year for the business community when new account books are opened. This Hindu festival of lights, also celebrates the homecoming of Lord Rama after a 14-year exile. There are fireworks everywhere.

Guru Nanak Jayanti is, on November 13, the birthday of the founder of Sikhism and a day of devotion by Bombay's Sikh community.

December: Christmas Day on December 25 is the celebration of the birth of Jesus Christ and accompanied by traditional exchanges of goodwill greetings and gifts.

The annual Chrysanthemum Festival is held at Delhi YMCA, Ashok Road.

Street Snack, Delhi

Practical Information

Festivals in Kashmir

In Srinagar, besides the national festivals of India, the following are local events.

April 13-14. Baisakhi is a festival marking the end of winter. It is also called the Blossom Festival. Srinagar's parks and gardens are crowded on these two days.

July-August. The Amar Nath Yatra is a pilgrimage trek held in high importance by Kashmiris. It starts from Pahalgam and thousands of pilgrims take up to five days to walk to the shrine of Lord Shiva in a cave to worship and ice lingham said to increase and lessen in size with the cycles of the moon.

Radio/Television

All India Radio and Television has some transmissions in English but programs begin and end at varying times. Check the newspapers.

Seminars

Details of seminars and workshops will be found in Delhi's English language daily press. Check for details.

Local Transport

Practical Information

GETTING AROUND DELHI

Delhi has a comprehensive public transport system of buses and electric trains. But the crowds on it can be a deterrent, particularly at peak periods.

Bus

The Delhi Transport Corporation operates on all routes on which places of tourist interest are situated. All day, all route tickets are available on Saturday and Sunday. There are also private or 'deluxe' buses which operate on a flat fare irrespective of the route or the distance travelled. The buses are quite reasonably maintained.

Train

Since 1982 Delhi has had a ring railway system known as the EMU which goes around the city on a regular schedule and covers both the major city stations and two suburban stations. Delhi's train system is worth trying but not at peak hours when hundreds of thousands of commuters are using the facility.

Taxis

While many taxis are metered, just as many are not. If the taxi has a meter, insist on it being flagged as soon as you enter. Where there is no meter in taxi or auto rickshaw, (a funny little three-wheeled vehicle which will be cheaper than a normal car,) ask to see the latest fare chart which the driver should have.

In some parts of Delhi, particularly Chandni Chowk, you can hire cycle-powered rickshaws which take only two passengers.

Taxis are plentiful in Delhi and can be hailed off the street. But if you want one that is air conditioned, order it from your hotel front desk or from the doorman outside. In the better class of hotel, the doorman controls incoming taxis and limousines with microphone and/or whistle.

> **INFOTIP:** If the taxi is unmetered and/or the driver does not speak English, ask your hotel doorman the fare you can expect to pay at your destination, and, if necessary, that he instruct the driver exactly where you want to go.

Always negotiate the fare on an unmetered taxi before you start off if you have flagged one down in the street. Do

Practical Information

not hire a tourist taxi or limousine for an excursion from an unlicenced or unapproved operator. GITO or your hotel will assist in finding a reputable firm. See Rental Vehicles with Drivers in this section. These firms have been approved by GITO.

If you are travelling by taxi late at night you may have difficulty in getting a driver to turn on the meter. Again insist on a price before you commence the trip.

GETTING AROUND OUTSIDE DELHI

By Road

As in Delhi itself, you can travel to its outskirts and well beyond by road by six methods.

1. Unmetered or private taxis. Fix rates in advance.
2. Metered taxis or auto rickshaws. Ask for the rate card in case the meter is not correctly calibrated for new rates, which is not uncommon.
3. Tourist cars/taxis, usually Indian Ambassador cars, which are quite comfortable and mostly chauffeur-driven by an English speaking driver. Some of these vehicles are air conditioned. Rates are reasonable and can be negotiated on an hourly or daily basis or for specific journeys. Alternatively the rate can be fixed per kilometre.
4. Limousine (luxury car/taxi.) These are imported air conditioned vehicles with English-speaking chauffeurs. The manner in which rates are determined is as above. These vehicles are available in Delhi and other major cities, but not in small towns.
5. Coaches for groups can be hired via the nearest Tourist Office.
6. 'Luxury' bus services to and from tourist centres. As schedules of these vehicles change, contact GITO for current departure times and places.

Complaints: Should you have a complaint against a taxi driver, telephone 2517403.

By Rail

There are five classes of accommodation in Indian trains but it is recommended that visitors travel First Class air conditioned or First Class which is about half price of air conditioned.

The **Indrail Pass** can be purchased with foreign currency by overseas visitors. This pass allows unlimited travel by rail within the period of validity. The pass is good value if you are travelling continuously.

Practical Information

> **INFOTIP:** As the Indrail Pass is issued on the basis of the class of travel, i.e. First Class Air Conditioned, it might be wise to ascertain if the trains you intent to use do in fact have air conditioned First Class carriages. If not, save and buy a normal First Class pass.

Holding a pass does not guarantee you a seat, so make a reservation. This comes without fee to pass holders, along with sleeper charges and supplementary charges for fast trains. Ordinary ticket-holders pay these fees. The time expended in gaining reservations can be frustrating. Make reservations up to six months in advance, if possible. If you book through a reputable travel agency with expertise in India, you can book your reservations in advance from home. A reservation ticket shows your seat/berth and carriage.

Meat Seller, Srinagar

Practical Information

Street Vendor

Do not expect Western First Class in sleeping compartments which usually transform into normal compartments by day. Bed rolls are provided in the AC class and on certain first class routes for a small fee, also in some second class sleepers. Tourists can reserve retiring rooms at railway stations for no more than 72 hours from occupation. Apply to individual station masters.

An Indrail Pass gives use of station waiting rooms - and their toilets. Use these in preference to those on board, which are often dirty.

Also available is the Indrail Rover Ticket for a selection of 32 itineraries of seven, 15, 21 and 30 days.

Practical Information

If you do not want an Indrail Pass or Rover Pass you can buy standard circular journey tickets which include a large number of stations. These are sold by each zonal railway and do away with the need to buy tickets at each stage.

Tickets can be bought and reservations made at the special railway booking office for foreign visitors, Northern Railway Reservation Office, Commercial Branch, Bardoda House, Curzon Rd, just opposite block K, Connaught Place. Tel: 45489. Here you can book for the Pink City Express to Jaipur, the Taj Express to Agra and the train to Jammu on the way to Srinagar. The Taj Express, departing New Delhi station, as distinct from Delhi station, returns on the same day from Agra.

For railway inquiries, ring the following telephone numbers. New Delhi, Delhi and Nizamuddin Stations - 3313535. For reservations, New Delhi, 344877; Delhi, 2513535.

For bookings on The Palace on Wheels through Rajathstan, contact Central Reservation Office, Rajasthan Tourism Development Corporation, Chandralok Building, 36 Janpath. Tel: 3321820. But to avoid disapppointment, make your reservations on this train in your home country through GITO or your travel agent.

For details and bookings of Indrail Passes contact the following general sales agents in your own country:

Australia: Adventure World Pty. Ltd., 37 York Street, Sydney, NSW, Tel: (02) 2903222: Penthouse Travel Pty. Ltd., 72 Pitt Street, Sydney, NSW, Tel: (02) 2311455.

Canada: Hariworld Travels Inc., Royal York Hotel, 100 Front Street West, Arcade Level, Toronto, Ontario M5J 1E3, Tel: 3662000.

Japan: Japan Travel Bureau, Overseas Travel Division, 1-6 - 4 Marunouchi, Chiyoda KU, Tokyo 100, Tel: 81 - (031) 2847391.

United Kingdom: S. D. Enterprises Ltd., 21 York House, Empire Way, Wembley, Middx, HA9 OPA, Tel: 019033411, 012009549.

USA: Hariworld Travels Inc., 30 Rockefeller Plaza, Shop 21, North Mezanine, New York, NY 10112, Tel: (212) 9573000.

Hong Kong: Thomas Cook Travel Servixces, 6/F D'Aguiler Place, 1-13, D'Aguiler St., Central, Hong Kong.

Practical Information

By Bus:

Generally in India bus travel is faster than rail, particularly, for example, on the Delhi - Jammu run.

It is preferable not to travel alone on a bus as close check should be maintained on luggage which is usually placed on top of the bus. Chai (tea) stops are frequent as indeed are unscheduled stops and there is a continuous stream of passengers taking luggage on and off. On some routes you can reserve a seat. At some bus stations there is a separate queue for women.

Inquiries: Interstate Bus Terminal, Kashmiri Gate, not for from the Delhi Railway Station in Old Delhi. Tel: 229083, also for information on bus transport in and around Old and New Delhi.

Driving Yourself:

Currently, India has no rental car facilities but they are planned soon to be introduced. Visitors may import their own vehicles but they must be covered by Triptyques or Carnets issued by an internationally recognised automobile association or club affiliated with the Alliance Internationale de Tourism, Geneva. Vehicles are allowed free of import duty for six months. Vehicles imported under Customs Carnets are permitted mainly for holiday-makers. The vehicle must be re-exported. Obtain an International Certificate for Motor Vehicles from your own country's automobile association or club, also an International Driving Permit.

Visitors intending to import a vehicle should write first to the Automobile Association of Upper India, Lilaram Building, 14-F, Connaught Place. Tel: 3312323.

A third party insurance is necessary for all vehicles (also canoes less than 5.5 metres long,) before use. Insurance must be paid to a company registered in India or a foreign company with a guarantor in India. In India, vehicles are driven on the left hand side of the road.

By Air:

If you are travelling large distances from Delhi, flying is undoubtedly the way to go. The Indian domestic airline, Indian Airlines, the largest carrier in south Asia, has an extensive network throughout the country. A second airline called Vayudoot also operates some services not previously included by Indian Airlines and duplicates others on high traffic routes.

Visitors to India must buy their air tickets in foreign currency. Indian Airlines has several special fares for

Practical Information

tourists from abroad. These include:

1. Discover India (21 days of unlimited travel provided no city is touched more than once except to transfer or connect.)

2. Tour India (Travel anywhere domestically for a maximum of six flights within 14 days. No city can be touched more than once, except to transfer or connect.)

3. India Wonderfares (Four fares each permitting unlimited travel for one week within north, south, east or west India regions.) No city can be touched more than once except to transfer or connect.

4. Youth Fares (25 per cent discount on US $ airfare on domestic and Indo - Nepal sectors for persons between 12 and 30 years of age.)

These economical packages can be bought abroad through Air India.

Reservations: Indian Airlines, Kanchenjunga Building, Barakhamba Rd. Tel: 3310071, 3310052, or Airport, 391250.

Reservations: Vayudoot Ltd., Malhotra Building, F Block, Janpath, New Delhi 110 001, Tel: 3312587, 3312779, 3315768. Palam Airport. Tel: 393544. Safdarjang Airport. Tel: 618271.

Air India also operates some internal flights between major cities, i.e. Delhi - Bombay.

Indira Gandhi International Airport is 18 km from central New Delhi. There are two domestic entrances, one for airbuses and one for international flights. There is also the smaller Safdarjang Airport, more centrally located. Some Vayudoot flights operate here.

At the international and domestic (not airbus) airports, GITO maintain offices to assist travellers, open 24 hours.

> **INFOTIP:** Should you have any problem with taxi drivers, note the number of the cab and report any incident to GITO or a member of the Traffic Police.

Passengers are required to pay a travel tax of 30 rupees before each internal flight and Foreign Travel Tax of 100R on leaving India. You can change money back into foreign currency at Indira Gandhi International Airport on production of exchange receipts.

Practical Information

Help!

Consulates/Embassies

Consular activities carried on by Embassies, High Commisions and consulates in Delhi are listed below. These services exist by agreement with the Government of India and are bound by certain Indian regulations, as well as by orders from their home countries.

Questions regarding:

> *Visas and passports*
> *Citizenship, dual nationality, national status*
> *Military service status of dual-nationality persons*
> *Difficulties with local regulations (Customs, the law, etc.)*
> *Assistance with absentee voting in home country*
> *Notarization or witnessing of documents*
> *Assistance in the case of a death*
> *Assistance with repatriation problems*

Embassies, High Commissions or Consulates are supposed to be notified in case of hospitalization of a foreigner, if the nationality of the patient is known.

Outside the Parliament House

Practical Information

In case of arrest in India, your embassy or consulate should be notified. Both Indians and foreigners are subject to the same laws in India and ignorance of the law is not a grounds for defence. However the consulate may inform you of your rights, notify your family, register complaints on your behalf and try to contact one of the Indian organisations that visit prisons and are concerned with the welfare of prisoners.

Australia: 1/50G, Shantipath, Chanakyapuri. Tel: 601336.
Austria: EP-13, Chandragupta Marg., Chanakyapuri. Tel: 601238.
Belgium: lock 50N, Shantipath, Chanakyapuri. Tel: 608295.
Canada: 7/8 Shantipath, Chanakyapuri. Tel: 608161.
Cyprus: 52 Jorbagh. Tel: 697503, 697508.
Denmark: 2, Golf Links. Tel: 616273.
Federal Republic of Germany: No. 6, Block 50G, Shantipath, Chanakyapuri. Tel: 644861.
Finland: Nyaya Marg., Chanakyapuri. Tel: 605409.
France: 2/50 E Shantipath, Chanakyapuri. Tel: 604004.
Greece: 16 Sunder Nagar. Tel: 617800.
Iceland: D-35, Pamposh Enclave. Tel: 6411027.
Indonesia: 50-A, Chanakyapuri. Tel: 602348.
Ireland: 13, Jor Bagh. Tel: 617435.
Italy: 13, Golf Links. Tel: 618311.

Practical Information

Japan: 50-G, Shantipath, Chanakyapuri. Tel: 604071.
Netherlands: 6/50 F Shantipath, hanakyapuri.
Tel: 609571.
New Zealand: 25, Golf Links. Tel: 697296.
Norway: Shantipath, Chanakyapuri. Tel: 605982.
Philippines: N/50, Nyaya Marg., Chanakyapuri.
Tel: 601120.
Portugal: B-76 Greater Kailash I. Tel: 6441206.
Singapore: E-61, Chandra Gupta Marg, Chanakyapuri.
Tel: 608149.
Yugoslavia: Vaswani Mansion, D. Wachha Rd, 222050/222373.
Spain: 12, Prithviraj Rd. Tel: 3015892.
Sweden: Nayaya Marg., Chanakyapuri. Tel: 604961.
United Kingdom: 50, Shantipath, Chanakyapuri.
Tel: 601371.
United States of America: Shantipath, Chanakyapuri.
Tel: 600651.
Yugoslavia: 3/50-G, Niti Marg., Chanakyapuri.
Tel: 606022.

Emergencies

Medical Emergencies

There are two important telephone numbers in Delhi for medical emergencies:

Ambulance: dial 102.
Police: 100.
Srinagar: Ambulance. Tel: 76992, 76835. Police: 100.

Most five, four and three star hotels have direct associations with a nearby medical practice and will assist in arranging a medical consultation in your hotel room should you become ill.
Hospitals and nursing homes in the Delhi central area are as follows:
Freemason's Polyclinic, Tolstoy Marg. Tel: 312929.
Gangaram Hospital, Gangaram Marg. Tel: 581837.
Hindu Rao Hospital, Hindu Rao Marg. Tel: 222522.
Holy Family Hospital, Okhla. Tel: 632355.
International Hospital, Chander Gupta d., Chanakyapuri.
Tel: 602189.
Kalawati Saran Children's Hospital, Bangla Sahib Rd.
Tel: 344106.
Lok Nayak Jaya Prakash Hospital, Jawaharial Nehru Marg.
Tel: 3311621.

Practical Information

Mool Chand K.R. Hospital, Lala Lajpat Rai Marg.
Tel: 611306.
Ram Manohar Lohia Hospital, Baba Kharak Singh Marg.
Tel: 321817.
Sir Ganga Ram Hospital, Ganga Ram Marg. Tel: 5712389.
Safdarjang Hospital, Sri Aurobindo Marg. Tel: 665060.
St Stephen's Hospital, Tees azari. Tel: 2511488.
Sucheta Kripalani Hospital, Panchkuin Marg. Tel: 343728.

If you must be admitted to hospital, your consulate will give advice on how to handle payment.

Should you require non-prescription medicines, or need to have a script made up from a doctor's prescription, here are several pharmacies to contact in Delhi:
Nath Brothers, 2 Marina Arcade, Connaught Circus.
Tel: 3327284.
Super Bazar Medical Store, Super Bazar, Connaught Circus (open 24 hours). Tel: 3310163.
Kemp and Co., 1E, Connaught Place. Tel: 3320329.
Popular Chemists, 2 Sunder Nagar Market. Tel: 619254.
Link Drug Store, G-5, South Extension Market, Part-1.
Tel: 625640.
Gainda Mull Hemraj, 11 Regal Building, Sansad Marg.
Tel: 353329.

Most Delhi pharmacies are closed on Sunday, but both Link Drug Store and Gainda Mull Hemraj open, the first between 9 a.m. and 7 p.m., the latter from 11.30 a.m. to 6 p.m.

Practical Information

Crime

Unfortunately, theft and pickpocketing are common. If you are a victim, try to recall as much detail as possible. It is rare for a stranger to be molested although it is unwise to wander around at night by yourself and to give alms to one person in a group of beggars. Be watchful of your luggage just before leaving a station. Sometimes, groups of thieves operate at this time, tossing bags from the train as it departs.

Should your driver be involved in a motor accident in a village outside Delhi, do not attempt to stop him from leaving the scene. Urge him to go to the nearest police station. Tempers run high if anyone is injured, so his escape is self-defence. The police will offer protection and also investigate. The police emergency telephone number is 100.

Death

A foreign visitor's death entails instant communication with his/her consulate by relatives, friends, hotel personnel, hospital or police authorities.

Lost Property

Should you lose something in your hotel, report it immediately to the hospitality desk if you are in a large hotel or front desk manager if in a smaller establishment. Otherwise contact the police.

Replacement of Items

In the event of losing your passport, report it to your consulate immediately. Guard your airline tickets as carefully as you would your cash. They will not be re-issued.

Credit Cards: Report the loss immediately to the crediut card company concerned. Check with your hotel's front desk for current address and telephone numbers in Delhi.

Travellers' Cheques: Lost or stolen travellers cheques are usually replaced quickly by the issuing banks or agents but the swiftness of replacement may depend on what proof you can supply, particularly cheque numbers and receipt for their purchase. Keep these in a separate place in your luggage away from your cheques.

Railway Passes: A lost railway pass may be replaced at

Practical Information

the discretion of the authority, particularly if the number of the pass can be confirmed with the railway office which issued it.

Libraries With Books In English

American Library, 24 Kasturba Gandhi Marg. Tel: 3314251. Closed Sunday.
British Council Library, Rafi Marg. Tel: 381401. Closed Sunday and Monday.
Bal Bhawan, Kotla Rd. Tel: 3317856. Closed Sunday and Monday.
IIC Library, 40 Lodi Eastate. Tel: 619431. Closed Sunday.
Nehru Library, Teen Murti House. Tel: 3015333. Closed Sunday.

Motoring

See also section on getting around India by road. While it is not possible yet to rent a self-drive car in Delhi.

Should you have your own vehicle, remember that throughout India traffic moves on the left side of the road and passes on the right side of a vehicle. There is no speed limit with the exception of 40 or 60 kilometres per hour as indicated in built- up city areas.

Most major roads are good but secondary roads are not of the same standards, particularly during the monsoon season.

Rental Vehicles With Drivers

There are many car hire firms in Delhi and a few in Srinagar. Most of them have offices inthe central Delhi area offering Ambassador cars, limousines and mini-coaches with drivers and with or without air conditioning. They include:

Indian Tourism Development Corporation, L-Block, Connaught Circus. Tel: 3320331.
I.S. Goal and Co., 16 Sunder Nager. Tel: 618755.
Travel House, 102 AVG Bhawan, M-3, Connaught Circus. Tel: 3323171.
Patna Sahib Tourist Corporation, 65 Regal Building, Connaught lace. Tel: 352024.
Karachi Taxi Co., 36 Janpath. Tel: 3323830.
Shikhar Travels, 209, Competent House, Connaught Place. Tel: 3312444.

Practical Information

Hindustan Tourist Taxi Service, 36 Janpath.

In Srinagar:
J & K Tourism Development Corporation, Tourist Reception Centre. Tel: 76107.
Srinagar Taxi Owners' Association, opposite Tourist Reception Centre. Tel: 74887.

> **INFOTIP:** On country roads and to a lesser extent, in Delhi, there is an unwritten rule that trucks, closely followed by buses, have right of way, even to pass in the face of oncoming traffic. This they do with alarming regularity, forcing all other types of transport from camel and ox-drawn carts to limousines off the road. Drive as do the Indians, using your car horn continuously and flashing your headlights. Be prepared to get out of the way quickly.

Publications in English

English Language Booksellers

Government of India Tourist Office, has plenty of literature in English on Delhi and most other parts of India.

Most five star hotels have a kiosk in which English language books, non-fiction and fiction, magazines and newspapers are for sale.

There are lots of very good bookshops in and around Connaught Place. These include the Oxford Book Shop, N Block, Connaught Place, New Book Depot at 18 Block, the English Book Depot and the Piccadilly Book Store, both also nearby.

Post Offices

Generally post and telegraph offices are open between 10 a.m. and 5 p.m. although there are services at the general post office outside of these hours. G.P.O. Old Delhi is on Mahatma Gandhi Rd., just west of the Yamuna Bridge. Tel: 2524369. New Delhi G.P.O. is at the intersection of Ashoka Rd., and Baba Karak Singh Marg. Tel: 344111. The Foreign Post Office is on Bahadur Shah Zafar Marg, just opposite the Dolls Museum: Tel: 3313304.

Practical Information

Other major city post offices include:
Connaught Place Post Office, A-Block. Tel: 344214.
Eastern Court Post Office, Janpath. Tel: 321878 (open 10 a.m. to 8 p.m. weekdays and 10 a.m. to 5 p.m. on Sundays and holidays.)
Post Restante is at GPO Ashoka Place. Tel: 322012. (open 8 a.m. to 7 p.m., weekdays. Closed Sundays and holidays.)
The Central Telegraph Office is at Eastern Court, Janpath. Tel: 311599.

For overseas telegrams and telephone calls go to the Overseas Communications Service, Bangla Sahib Rd. Open 24 hours daily.

> **INFOTIP:** Envelopes on sale or available through your hotel are short on back adhering material. Glue is provided at most post offices but to make sure your letter is sealed, buy a roll of cellulose tape for more security.

Smaller post and telegraph offices are contained in most 5-star hotels. If not, the front desks of most 5 and 4 star hotels offer postal facilities for guests. Indira Gandhi International Airport has a post office.

International telegraph inquiries. Tel: 312254.

Srinagar: GPO, The Bund. Tel: 76494. Also there is a PO at the airport. Tel: 31521. The Central Telegraph Office is on Maulana Azad Rd and is open 24 hours daily. Tel: 76549.

Religious Services in English

Catholic

Cathedral of the Sacred Heart, Ashoka Place, GPO. Tel: 343593.
St. Mary's Church, S.P. Mukherjee Marg. Tel: 2527540. Sunday Mass in English, 9.30 a.m.
St Michael's Church, Prasad Nagar. Tel: 5717657. Sunday Mass in English, 8.30 a.m. and 6 p.m.
Vatican Embassy Chapel, 50-C Niti Marg., Chanakyapuri. Tel: 606921. Mass in English, 6.30 p.m. weekdays only.

Protestant

Cathedral Church of the Redemptioon, Church Rd. Tel: 3015396. Sunday English service, 8 a.m.

Practical Information

Centenary Methodist Church, Lala Lajpat ai Marg. Tel: 362441. English Sunday service, 8 a.m.
Free Church, 10, Jantar Mantar Rd. Tel: 311331. Sunday English services, 10 a.m. and 5.30 p.m.
Green Park Free Church, A-24, Green Park. Tel: 664574. Sunday service in English, 9.30 a.m.
Seven-Day Adventists, 11 Hailey Rd. English services, Tuesday, 7 p.m., Friday, 7 p.m.
St. Thomas Church, 59 Mandir Marg. Sunday service in English, 8 a.m.

Jewish

Services may not be conducted in English.
Jewish Community Hall, 2 Humayun Rd.

Srinagar Catholic Church, Maulana Azad Rd.
Protestant Church, Munshi Bagh.

Restaurants and Nightlife

While Delhi offers all of the distinctive regional cuisines of the nation and also continental, Chinese and some Asian, it specialises in marvellous mughlai and tandoori dishes. These are often served in restaurants advertising Frontier Food. No matter the label, the fare is sure to be good.

Naturally, where 'Indian' menus are offered, it generally means North Indian. You will also find Kashmiri cuisine included in the menus of several establishments which advise they serve Indian or North Indian. So eat heartily though wean your system on to the spicier dishes if you are not used to them.

Prices, even in the five-star establishments, by western standards, are inexpensive and a good, non-hotel, simple eatery can provide terrific value for very little.

While it is believed that India's national dish is curry and rice, there is no such single thing as curry. It's as general as the word sauce. Curry is a combination of freshly ground spices, each able to be varied in intensity of palate heat and subtlety of flavour and combined with meat, fish, poultry or vegetables and, occasionally, fruit. Indian cooks may select from about 25 different spices and many herbs to make what westerners recognize as curry. Many of the recipes are closely guarded secrets handed down from generation to generation. Spices are ground freshly or used whole.

Practical Information

Many of the top class hotels produce excellent European food and also authentic fare from other parts of Asia. But you won't be able to get a steak because the cow is sacred. A reasonable alternative in a few establishments is the buffalo steak and your hamburger is likely to be lamburger or burger made from ham as from the pig. The latter meat is considered unclean by Muslims.

> **INFOTIP:** If dining with a Muslim in a restaurant where pork is on the menu, ask if your choice of it will offend. If you think it might, opt for another type of meat.

Not all Hindus are strict vegetarians but because many are, it is likely you'll end up discovering a whole new world of vegetables in India. A strict Buddhist will not even eat eggs.

Fatehpur Sikri, near Agra

Brass Seller, Srinagar

BREAKFAST: Most hotels serve western breakfast, continental and/or cooked with, often, a goodly selection of fruits as well. The toast might not be as you'd prepare it yourself and the bacon might be done to a crisp as Americans prefer it. (Specify otherwise if you don't like this.) The milk for your tea or coffee might be boiled and hot but it will be safe to drink. Otherwise you may be given powdered creamer. Generally, western breakfasts are hearty and good value. Delhi's Hotel Ashok, for instance, serves the most marvellous chicken livers on toast imagineable!

You might like to try Indian-style breakfast, perhaps masala dosa, vegetable-stuffed pancakes served with pickles on a banana leaf, or rice with vegetables and pickles. These make interesting changes and hotels have selections on their menus for their Indian guests.

Some hotels have 24-hour coffee shops in which case you'll have no problem in gaining breakfast if you have to be on the move before 7 a.m. when most hotel dining rooms open for the first repast of the day. An alternative is 24-hour room service but you may find that only tea and coffee are available before this hour.

LUNCH AND DINNER: The Delhi locals start lunching between noon and 12.30 p.m. in restaurants, hotel or otherwise, and at any time from street vendors. Some (not in hotels) open as early as 11 a.m. and all continue till 3 p.m. at least. While many restaurants open for dinner from 7 to 7.30 p.m., those located in hotels tend to open at either 7.30 or 8 p.m.

Because of the diversity of food in Delhi, here is a resume of the regional styles you are likely to encounter in hotel, restaurant or street stall.

Northern Indian

The hearty food of the north has Muslim then Mughal influences resulting in the variety of savoury, rich lamb dishes based on cooking with ghee and cream. The cuisine was enhanced by the tandoor method of cooking which was indigenous to the north west frontier province, now Pakistan, and the Punjab. The tandoor is a clay oven which burns wood or charcoal and imparts an unparalleled smoky flavour to mildly-spiced, tender meats, fish, poultry and breads.

Punjabi food is simple and filling, an amalgamation of the cuisines of the Greeks, Persians, Afghans and Mongols, plus northern invaders. Ghee, fresh milk products and vegetables are utilized.

If you see a restaurant advertizing Frontier Food, it is likely to include tandoor and Punjabi food and is well worth experiencing. Here are some dishes to try:

Naan: Leavened flour bread
Biriyani: Rice, saffron and marinated lamb
Kabab: Meat, poultry or fish served on a skewer with accompaniments such as tomatoes, onion, capsicum.
Murgh: Chicken. Murgh tikka should be melt-in-the-mouth tandoori chicken morsels on a kebab.
Paneer: Cottage cheese. Palek Paneer is the cheese, spices, onion and tomato served with spinach. Matter paneer is with peas.
Pillau: Spiced rice
Keema: Minced meat
Roghan Josh: Lamb with spices in yoghurt

Practical Information

Authentic north Indian fare can be found at the dhabas, small street eating places dotted around the city and along highways to serve motorists.

Maharashtrian

The cuisine of the State of which Bombay is capital is healthy and emphasizes wheat, rice, vegetables (many of the people are vegetarian,) nuts and nut oils, sesame seeds and coconut. Often, vegetables are spiced with a combination of ground and roasted cumin, sesame seeds, cardamom, cinnamon and coconut. Bombay Duck is Maharashtrian and is a little fish pickled, stewed or fried. Sweet and sour dishes are also interesting eating. Specialties include Bhel puri: Boiled potatoes, onion, fresh coriander, crisp wheat, puffed rice served with chutneys and chick pea vermicelli.

Gujarati

From the State of Gujarat comes an interesting vegetarian cuisine, usually served thali style, ie on a tray with each different dish served in small stainless-steel bowls - a mini smorgasbord. The food is oil free and not pungent and the waiters keep filling up the thali bowls until you are replete. The cuisine is a trifle sweet and desserts, made often with milk and/or yoghurt, are special. To contrast, the Gujaratis are big on pickles and relishes.

Khandvi: Gram flour paste steamed rolls with mustard seed and fresh coriander.
Dhoklas: Steamed lentil cakes.

Note: Not all thali-food is vegetarian. It is a style of presentation rather than cuisine. Embracing several styles, a typical thali meal is meat, chicken or fish, two vegetable dishes, dhal or lentils pureed, raita (yoghurt mixed with cucumber or other vegetables to refresh the palate,) pickles or chutney and perhaps one of the breads - naan, papadams, roti or chapatti. Rice is also served.

Parsi

While Parsi food is heavily spiced, it is not overly hot which makes it a favourite with many foreigners. With a Persian heritage, the Parsis are into meat and fish and eggs. (If a Parsi is stumped for a culinary idea, he/she adds eggs.)

Practical Information

Dhansak: Traditionally eaten on Sundays, cooked in a mixture of several dhals (lentil sauces, common to many of India's cuisines,) chicken or lamb comes with deep fried meat balls and caramelized brown rice.

Patra-ni-Machini: Served on special occasions is this pomfret (fish) fillet, stuffed with coriander and coconut chutney and steamed in a banana leaf.

Sindhi

The Sindhis are a people who migrated from Pakistan after 1947 petition, bringing with them a little-known cuisine characterized by garlic and mint flavoured chutneys and pickles and sweets like mithais and hashwas. Food is not necessarily vegetarian.

Kofta Tas-Me: Meat balls in sauce of onion, tomato, chilli, ginger, coriander and sprinkled with garam masala.

Bengali

Fish, particularly freshwater, seafood, mustard seed and oil (grown in the region) dominate the Bengali diet which is rejecting of sea fish. Fish is stewed, grilled or fried. While yoghurt is rarely offered separately, it is used sometimes in preparation. A speciality from the days of the Raj is marinated hilsa but, beware, it has lots of bones. The Bengalis love sweetmeats.

Murhu Ghonta: Classic Bengali fish head, spicy.
Maacher Jhol: Lightly fried fish in a gravy westerners would classify as curry.

South Indian

In the south, one finds a Brahmin cuisine, distinctive because strict south Indian Brahmins will not eat tomatoes and beetroot because they are blood colour and neither onion nor garlic. Recipes are based on tamarind, chilli, coconut and yellow lentil. These combined with a vegetable make sambhar, a staple dish eaten twice daily with rasama, a peppery, lentil based consumee and the basis of the English-inspired mulligatawny. With rice, vegetables, coconut and yoghurt, you have a typical meal.

The popularity of idlis and dosas, respectively steamed dumplings and pancakes made from fermented ground rice and dhal, has spread throughout the nation. Yet Moghul influences from Hyderabad, also those of Christian, Syrian, and Jewish origin are also prominent in the food and meat and seafood are enjoyed also by non-vegetarians. Some dishes can be exceedingly hot to western palates.

Haleem: Wheat and mutton.
Hyderabad biryani: Rice with meat.
Baghara baigan: Eggplant dish.

Goan

The Christian Portguese had a great influence on Goan cuisines as did the Muslims. Traditions of Christians using vinegar, Hindus lokum, a sour fruit and tamarind, to give pungency, combine with the Christian preference for pork and the non- vegetarian Hindus liking for lamb. Seafood and fish are bountiful. Goan sausages are richly individual (rather salty.)

Vindaloo: Meat in garlic spices and vinegar. (Whoosh! Have plenty of water ready.)
Sorpatel: Pork in a similar combo.
Fish or seafood curries: Self explanatory and very good.

Kashmiri

The most interesting and ceremonial of Kashmiri meals is the Wazwan, a procession of many dishes served to guests seated on the floor. The chief cook or waza supervises the serving of each. It is usually conducted in a private home. A variety of delicacies such as roganjosh, kebabs and vegetables - usually about 12 dishes but up to 32 for a grand occasion - is presented, concluding with gushtaba a dessert called phirni then a cup of kahwah, Kashmiri green tea flavoured with saffron, cardamom and almonds. One eats by hand (the right) then male Kashmiris usually settle tdown to talk over their hookahs or water pipes.

Alcoholic Drinks

In Delhi, there is partial prohibition of alcohol. While some visitors can travel in and out, drink alcohol freely in hotels and even buy it without being questioned in liquor stores, others may be asked to produce their All India Liquor Permits at the latter. Beer can be bought without the permit.

Residents of reputable hotels, guests in private homes and clubs in which members have permits, should not need to produce a permit. But certain national holidays and

Practical Information

frequently, Fridays, are observed as 'dry' days in some, but not all establishments in Delhi. Inquire.

It is not traditional for alcohol to be served in other than westernized Indian homes and some restaurants serve only beer, in addition to fruit juices and water. Imported spirits and wines are served in top hotel restaurants but at astronomical prices.

Some Indian maitre d's seem rather reluctant to admit that India produces its own wine and spirits. Some of the wine is surprisingly good and some of it awful but so is imported wine that has tainted while waiting to be unloaded from a slow moving wharf or bond store. The spirits, while some are a bit rough around the edges, are fine with mixers and much cheaper.

A Break for Kashmiri tea

Practical Information

Embroiderers

Craftsman

> **INFOTIP:** If you forget or run out of your duty-free and don't want to pay the high prices for mini-bar nips in your room, get a taxi driver to take you to an Indian liquor store. You may be asked to produce a permit. The prices for Indian-produced products are very reasonable, not so imports.

You can buy Indian wines in good hotels by the glass or bottle. It is still fairly expensive in a flashy place but less than imported.

Regional and International Restaurants

Indian

(Restaurants listed may have one or a combination of Northern Indian, Tandoori or North West Frontier Food food.)

Darbar, Hotel Ashok, 50B Chanakyapuri. Tel: 600121. Indian and Mughlai. Speciality, Raan Aleeshaan, tandoor-baked lamb leg marinated in rum and spices. Meat lovers' delight. Some vegetarian. Reasonably priced. Evening entertainment. Reservations.

Frontier, Hotel Ashok, address and telephone as above. Very hearty frontier food. Popular with families.

Kandahar, Hotel Oberoi, Dr. Zakir Hussain Marg. Tel: 363030. Very good tandoor dishes. Reservations.

Handi, Taj Palace Hotel, Sardar Patel Marg, Diplomatic Enclave. Tel: 3010404. Northern and western Indian specialties. Intimate atmosphere. Evenings, classical Indian music. Reservations.

Bukhara, Maurya Sheraton Hotel, Diplomatic Enclave. Tel: 3010101. Barbecued specialties from the North West Frontier. Reservations.

Bara-dari, Samrat Hotel, Chanakyapuri. Tel: 603030. Great Muglai plus Kashmiri food.

Aangan, Hyatt Regency Hotel, Bhikaji Cama, Ring Rd. Tel: 609911. Traditional North Indian specialties. Reservations.

The Panorama, Kanishka Hotel, 19 Ashok Rd. Tel: 343400. Top floor with excellent views. Indian and continental. Excellent vegetarian.

Dhaba, Claridges Hotel, 12 Aurangzeb Rd. Tel: 3010211. Reservations.

Daawat, Sartaj Hotel, A-3, Green Park. Tel: 663277. Indian and Mughlai, plus Chinese and continental.

Dasaprakash, Hotel Ambassador complex, Sujan Singh Park. Tel: 694966. Vegetarian only, including South Indian.

Practical Information

Gulati, 6 Pandara Road Market, near India Gate.
Tel: 38839. Light music.

Lido Restaurant, M-37 Connaught Circus. Tel: 3329780.
Open 5 p.m. to midnight. Also continental food. Caberet shows 6 p.m. to 10 p.m.

In the old quarters of the Mughal city are many restaurants around Jama Masjid. They serve authentic mughlai cuisine in plain surroundings and include:

Flora, Urdu Bazar, Jama Masjid, Old Delhi. Tel: 264593.

Moti Mahal, Moti Nagar, Daryaganj. Tel: 273011.

Karim, Jama Masjid, Old Delhi. Tel: 269880.

Similar food is served at the following in New Delhi:

Degchi, 13 Regal Building, Connaught Place. Tel: 311444.

Mughlai, M-17, Connaught Circus. Tel: 3321101.

Tandoori Club, M Block, Greater Kailash II. Tel: 6430658.

South Indian

Woodlands, Hotel Lodhi, Lala Lajpat Rai Marg.
Tel: 362422.

Coconut Grove, Ashok Yatri Niwas Hotel, 19 Ashok Rd.
Tel: 3324511. Non-vegetarian.

Sona Rupa, 46 Janpath. Tel: 3326807.

French

Burgundy, Ashok Hotel, 50 B, Chanakyapuri. Tel: 600121.
Intimate atmosphere. Evening entertainment. Top cuisine. Reservations.

La Rochelle, The Oberoi Hotel, Dr. Zakir Hussain Marg.
Tel: 699571. Gracious atmosphere. Reservations.

Takshila, Maurya Sheraton, Diplomatic Enclave.
Tel: 3010101. Also includes other Mediterranean dishes. Charming environment. Reservations.

Le Parisien, Hotel Sofitel Surya, Friends Colony.
Tel: 635070. Specialised French. Reservations.

Rajasthani Woman

Restaurant de France, Le Meridien Hotel, Windsor Place.
Tel: 383960. Reservations.

Italians Valentino's, Hyatt Regency, Bhikaji Carma Place.
Tel: 609911. Reservations.

Casa Medici, Taj Mahal Hotel, 1, Mansingh Rd.
Tel: 3016162. Rooftop with fine views. Reservations.

Chinese

Chinatown, Ashok Hotel, 50B Chanakyapuri. Tel: 600121.
Szechuan and Cantonese. Up-marketplace atmosphere.
Good selections. Reservations.

Jade Garden, Claridges Hotel, 12 Aurangzeb Rd.
Tel: 3010211. Szechuan cuisine.

Pearls, Hyatt Regency Hotel, Bhikaji Carma, Ring Rd.
Tel: 609911. Szechuan specialities. Reservations.

Shaolin, Hotel Centaur, Delhi Airport. Tel: 391411.

Practical Information

Far Eastern Restaurant, Holiday Inn, Barakhamba Ave., Connaught Place. Tel: 3316911. Szechuan too.

Mandarin Room, Janpath Hotel, Janpath. Tel: 350070. Dancing each evening.

Golden Phoenix, Le Meridien Hotel, Windsor Place. Tel: 383960. Cantonese and Szechuan. Reservations.

Chinese Room, Nirula's Hotel, L-Block, Coonaught Circus. Tel: 352419.

Sampan, Sofitel Surya Hotel, Friends Colony. Tel: 63570. Rooftop restaurant and nightclub, also featuring some Polynesian dishes.

House of Ming, Taj Mahal Hotel, 1 Mansingh Rd. Tel: 3016162. Szechuan and Cantonese in admirable surrounds. Reservations.

Tea House of the August Moon, Taj Palace Hotel, Sardar Patel Marg, Diplomatic Enclave. Tel: 3010404. Includes dim sum tea house service. Reservations.

Taipan, The Oberoi Hotel, Dr. Zakir Hussain Marg. Tel: 699571. Szechuan. Magnificent original, old Chinese watercolours add to the atmosphere. Reservations.

Japanese

Tokyo, Hotel Ashok, 50B Chanakyapuri. Tel: 600121. Delhi's only Japanese-only-cuisine restaurant. Others combine Japanese with other cuisines. Authentic. Sake available. Western and Japanese seating. Reservations.
Fujiya Restaurant, 12-48-Malcha Marg. Tel: 3016059.

Sakura, Hotel Vikram, Ring Rd. Tel: 6436451. A few Japanese dishes plus Chinese and continental.

Western Fast Foods

Nirula's, L-Block, Coonaught Circus. Tel: 3322419.

The Treat, Palika Underground Parking Complex. Tel: 322295.

American Pie, Asian Games Village Complex. Tel 6447230.

The Pizza 'N' Pizza, 64, Scindia House. Tel: 3322219.

Practical Information

The following hotels have 24-hour coffee shops, useful if one has an early morning or late night departure and offering a range of meals and snacks, usually representing Indian, continental and sometimes Chinese dishes, no matter the hour.

Samovar, Hotel Ashok
24 Hotel Coffee Shop, Hotel Centaur
Pickwick's, Claridges Hotel
Cafe Promenade, Hyatt Regency
Holiday Inn 24-hour Restaurant
Open House, Hotel Janpath
La Barasserie, Le Meridien Hotel
Gardenia, Samrat Hotel
Lubbini, Siddharth Hotel
Le Cafe, Sofitel Surya Hotel
Machan, Taj Mahal Hotel
Isfahan, Taj Palace Hotel
The Palms, The Oberoi Hotel
Vasant Continental Hotel 24-hour Coffee Shop and The Pavilion, Hotel Maurya Sheraton.

Night Life

In addition to the theatre and cultural programmes often scheduled with dinner at intermittant times by hotels, there are a few discos starting from between 9.30 p.m. and 10.30 p.m. and finishing at between 3 a.m. and 4 a.m. or whenever the guests want to leave!

> **INFOTIP:** Delhi discos tend to be very exclusive places, needing membership which is difficult and quite expensive to acquire or that one is a guest of the hotel in which the disco is incorporated. If you are into discos, choose to stay at one of the following hotels or else find an Indian friend who is a member and can sign you in.

Oasis Disco, Hyatt Regency Hotel
Number One, Taj Mahal Hotel
Ghungroo Disco, Maurya Sheraton Hotel
Copacabana, Le Meridien
Hotel and Sampan Nightclub, Sofitel Surya Hotel

In addition to the above, the Hotel Oberoi's Connaught Bar has dancing to a band at night. Membership is not needed.

Practical Information

Srinagar

Restaurants and Night Life

As Kashmir is very much a tourist resort, cultural programmes vary according to the season, so inquire of the Government Tourist Offices when and where these are likely to be, particularly in conjunction with dinner at a hotel.

As so many guests stay on houseboats on a full-board or half- board basis and are catered-for, with an option being a packed lunch if they have a day excursion, lots do not venture into the restaurants of Srinagar. But there are many in which can be judged externally and by a quick look inside.

The Oberoi Palace Hotel, Gupkar Road,(Tel 75617) welcomes non- residents for lunch and dinner, the former of which can be partaken on the spacious lake-viewing lawns or in the dining room. In the garden is a small but very good lunch selection of Indian, Mughlai and Kashmiri food. The dining room menu is larger and serves similar cuisines in this former palace.

Hotel Centaur, Chashmeshahi with lake views (tel: 71215) has the Dawatkhana Indian restaurant and a 24-hour coffee shop.

See also Kashmir sidetrip.

Shopping

Delhi has a plethora of fascinating goods to tempt the most discerning of shoppers. These include hand-crafted items, jewellery, pottery, brass, copper and silverware, fabrics (from cotton to silks,) traditional and trendy ready-made garments and all things leather.

You can buy goods from almost every State of India at their government emporia and all goods at these stores are at fixed prices. While excellent shopping can be done in the main shopping arcades, some of the most exciting bargains are in the bazaars on and off Janpath in small alleys.

In these, as in Chandni Chowk, Sadar Bazar and Nehru Place, one must bargain enthusiastically. These shopping areas plus Palika Bazar and Shankar Market, both at Connaught Place, are closed Sundays.

Ajmal Khan Market, INA, Defence Colony, Khan Market, South Extension, Lajpatnagar and Yashvant Place (Chanakyapuri) are closed Mondays. Green Park Hauz

Khas, Greater Kailash, Vasant Vihar and Safdarjang Enclave market and shopping areas are closed Tuesdays.

Shops, especially government emporia, are usually open from 10 a.m. to 7 p.m. with an hour or more for lunch.

Genuine antiques are hard to find but the market in Sunder Nagar has several stores with interesting objets d'art.

Hotels and Archana Shopping Arcade in Greater Kailash I have good boutiques for men, women and children and, in addition to buying Kashmiri carpets, others can be ready-made. Many hotels have good carpet shops. Furniture can be bought or made to order.

The State Emporia complex at Baba Kharak Singh Marg, just down from Radial Road 2 at Connaught Place, represents the handicrafts of all States of India. These are from Andra Pradesh, Assam, Bihar, Gujarat, Haryana, Himachal Pradesh, Karnataka. Kashmir, Kerala, Madhya Pradesh, Manipur, Maharashtra, Nagaland, Orissa, Punjab, Rajasthan, Tamil Nadu, Tripura, Utter Pradesh and West Bengal.

Government Emporia

Central Cottage Industries Emporium, Janpath.
Tel: 311506.
Also at Gandhi Ashram Khadi Bhandar, 42-H, Connaught Place. Tel: 321077.
Handloom House, 9A Connaught Place. Tel: 3443506.
Handicrafts and Handloom Export Corporation Showroom, Lok Kalyan Bhawan, 11A Rouse Avenue Lane.
Tel: 3311086.
Kashmir Government Arts Emporium, 5 Prithvi Raj Rd.
Tel: 611096.
Also at 22B, Connaught Place. Tel: 320581.
Also Khadi Gramodyog Bhawan, 24 Regal Building.
Tel: 310902.
Also Super Bazar, Connaught Circus. Tel: 40163.

Kashmir Shopping

Kashmir's handicrafts, principally its carpets, silk and wool, materials and clothing are world famous, and the State's craftsmen also produce unique articles in wood and papier mache. In Srinagar, the main shopping areas are Boulevard, Budshah Chowk, Hari Singh High Street, Lal Chowk, Maulana Azad Road and Residency Road. The following are addresses of government emporia in **Srinagar:**

Practical Information

Kashmir Government Arts Emporium, Shervani Rd.
Tel: 73011.
Also at Government Central Market, Boulevard.
Tel: 77466.
Rajasthan Emporium, Shervani Rd.
UPICA, UP Handlooms, Poloview. Tel: 75850.
Shri Gandhi Ashram Khadi Bahandar, Shervani Rd.
Tel: 73321.

Excellent walnut furniture at very reasonable prices can be found at **Langoo and Co, Anzimar, Khanyar**. Tel: 78860. Here are also the prized pashmina and shahtush shawls, as soft as whispers, embroideries, silks, shawls and saris. **Mr H.M. Sadiq, Hassan Abad Rainawari** (accessible by shikara) will point out the difference between the inferior and quality papier mache goods which he makes, even if one does not want to buy. Tel: 72720.

Houseboat owners **Reshu Boktoo & Sons** have a quality carpet outlet at Dal Gate, just by their new hotel.

Shop in **Agra** and **Jaipur** on sidetrips for semi-precious stones inlaid into marble boxes and trays and also fabulous jewellery and precious stones.

Musical Instruments

Indian musical instruments are very popular purchases with foreign visitors. Government approved stores selling them in Delhi are:
Lahare Music House, Daryaganj. Tel: 271305.
A. Godin & Co., 1 Regal Building, Connaught Place.
Tel: 312809.
Rikhi Ram, 8 Marina Arcade, Connaught Circus.
Tel: 344385.

The GITO keeps detailed lists of shops it recommends in Delhi and several other tourist centres.

> **INFOTIP:** Check with GITO on the reliability of the stores offering to freight items to your home address.

Major hotels have shops but expect to pay more. **Bazaars are open from 10 a.m. till 9 p.m.** Credit cards and travellers' cheques are accepted at government emporia and the bigger shops but pay cash in the bazaars.

ITDC also operates a duty-free shop at Indira Gandhi International Airport. There are book and souvenir shops at both airports.

Practical Information

Antiquities

Antiquities and objets d'art more than 100 years old are banned from being taken out of India. It is also prohibited that any skins of animals, including snakes, and the products made from them, used or unused, are included in accompanied or unaccompanied baggage.

To discover if purchases are antiquities or not contact the *Director Antiquities*, Archaeological Survey of India, Janpath, New Delhi -110 001, Superintendent Archaeologist, *Antiquities, Archaeological Survey* of India, Sion Fort, Bombay, Superintending Archaeologist, *Eastern Circle*, Archaeological Survey of India, Narayani Building, Brabourne Road, Calcutta - 700 013; Superintending Archaeologist, *Southern Circle*, Archaeological Survey of India, Fort St. George, Madras - 600 001 or Superintending Archaeologist, *Frontier Circle*, Archaeological Survey of India, Minto Bridge, Srinagar, Kashmir.

Carved horses head, Antique

Practical Information

Sports and Athletics

BALLOONING: Ballooning Club of India, Safdarjang Airport.

BOATING: Delhi Boating Club, Rafi Marg, India Gate Lawns. Tel: 3310995.

BOWLING: The Qutab Hotel, off Sri Aurabindo Marg, has a public, four-lane 10-pin bowling facility. Tel: 660060.

FISHING: Keen fishermen can try their luck close to Delhi. Badhkal Lake is 32 km distant with fishing permit available on the spot. Ballabgarh Lake is 36.8 km from Delhi on the Agra Highway. Okhla, only 11.8 km from the city on the Delhi- Mathura Road also has fishing. Fishing permits are available from the GITO at 88 Janpath.

FLYING: The Delhi Flying Club at Safdarjang Airport offers a monthly membership for a fee. Tel: 699596.

GLIDING: Delhi Gliding Club, Safdarjang Airport.
Tel: 611298.

GOLF: Delhi Golf Club, Dr. Zakir Hussain Marg, (next to Oberoi Hotel.) Tel: 360002. (One 18-hole championship course and one nine-hole practice course. Casual players welcomed. Open from 6 a.m. to 6 p.m. all week.)
There is also a floodlit golf driving range at the Siri Fort Sports Complex. Casual membership available. Open 10 a.m. to 2 p.m. for casual players.
Hotel Centaur, Delhi Airport has a golf putting green. Tel:391411.
Miniature golf is at the Holiday Inn, Barakhamba Avenue, Connaught Place. Tel: 3316911. Also Ashok Hotel, Chankyapuri. Tel: 600121.

HANG GLIDING: Hang Gliding Club of India, Safdarjang Airport.

HORSE RIDING: Delhi Riding Club, Safdarjang Rd.
Tel: 3011891.

POLO: President's Estate Polo Club, Rashtrapati Bhavan. Tel: 3015604.

SAILING: Defence Services Sailing Club, Okhla.
Tel: 3019604.

Practical Information

TENNIS: Delhi Lawn Tennis Association, Africa Avenue. Tel: 666140. The following 5-star hotels have tennis facilities for guests:

Centaur Hotel, Claridges Hotel, Hyatt Regency and Maurya Sheraton.

SQUASH: The Holiday Inn Hotel, Barakhamba Avenue, Connaught Place. Tel: 3316911.

SWIMMING: There are public swimming pools at Talkatora Gardens, Talkatora Road and at Nehru Park, near the Hotel Ashok.

Most five and some four-star hotels in Delhi have swimming pools and health clubs for guests.

Spectator Sports

For all spectator sports - cricket, hockey, horse racing, rugby, soccer etc., contact GITO, Tel: 3320005 for dates and times of meetings. Also consult Daily Delhi English-language newspapers.

YOGA: Yoga classes are held at Vishwayatan, Ashok Rd. Tel: 388866, weekdays from 4.30 p.m. to 6 p.m.

Some hotels have yoga classes in their health clubs.

Chandni Chowk, rickshaws

Practical Information

Fabric Markets in Delhi

Sports In Kashmir (Srinagar)

BADMINTON: Oberoi Palace Hotel, Gupkar Rd., Srinagar. Tel: 71241.

BILLIARDS: Amar Singh Club. Tel: 76848.
Srinagar Club. Tel: 72132. (Temporary memberships at both clubs.)

BOATING: Watersports Institute, Nagin Lake.
Tel: 76517.

GOLF: Kashmir Government Golf Club, Maulana Azad Rd. Tel: 76524.(Temporary daily or monthly membership and equipment for hire.) 18 holes.
Palace Golf Course, Boulevard. 6-hole beginners' course. The Oberoi Palace Hotel, Gupkar Rd.Tel: 71241. Putting green and Mini golf course.

FISHING: Kashmir offers wonderful lake and river fishing. Permits from the Directorate of Fisheries, Tourist Reception Centre, Srinagar. Tel: 72862. Fishing equipment can be hired. Check for dealers with your hotel desk or houseboat host.

SKIING: Gulmarg, about 60 km from Srinagar, is India's snow skiing capital. It has several hotels. Ski facilities include t-bar chair lift. The Gulmarg Ski School organizes tuition and also water skiing on Lakes Dal and Nagin in summer.

SQUASH AND TENNIS: Amar Singh Club. Tel: 76848. Temporary memberships available.

SWIMMING: Water Sports Institute, Lake Nagin.
Tel: 76517. The Hotel Broadway and the Centaur Lakeview Hotel have swimming pools for guests.

TREEKING: Two trekking maps are available from the Tourist Reception Centre in Srinagar, giving details of routes. Trekking equipment can be rented from the Department of Tourism, Tourist Reception Centre and J & K Government Tourist Office. Tel: 71921. Route maps also available from J & K Tourist Offices in New Delhi, Bombay, Calcutta, Madras, Hyderabad, Ahmedabad and Jammu Tawi.

Several private operators offer very good trekking packages. One reliable company is Reshu Boktoo & Sons,

Practical Information

Suilman Shopping Complex, Dal Gate, 77579. The company also has water trekking and fishing tours by shikhara.

The New Delhi office is Shop G, Shopping Arcade, Connaught Palace Hotel, 37 Shaheed Bhagat Singh Marg. Tel: 344952.

WATER SKIING: Water Sports Institute, Nagin Lake. Tel: 76517.

Spectators Sports

These are held in Srinagar's two main stadia; Bakshi Stadium, Hazuri Bagh. Tel: 71014 and at the Sher-i-Kashmir Sports Complex, also on Hazuri Marg. For dates and times, inquire at J & K Tourist Reception Centres or consult your hotel or houseboat staff.

Telephone and Telegraph

Neither Delhi, Srinagar, Agra or Jaipur have a system of public telephone booths operated by the government to the same extent of most western countries. However, many small businesses connected by telephone offer the use of this phone to the visiting public for a fee usually double that of a local call from a public booth which is currently 50 paise. Internally, long distance telephone calls can be very frustrating to the tourist. The government is progressively updating the system but be prepared for long delays when booking a call and a connection that can sound as if you are speaking to someone on the moon.

International calls are also subject to long delays - it can be hours - although most five-star deluxe, five star and four star hotels have direct dialling facilities from guest rooms. You can place a collect call from India to the following countries: Australia, Belgium, Canada, France, Israel, Japan, Kuwait, Maldives, New Zealand, Norway, South Korea, Sweden, Switzerland, United Kingdom, USA, Spain, Thailand and West Germany. Expect to pay a service charge for the placing of a collect call.

On some deluxe houseboat on Srinagar's lakes, you can make and receive calls from the land base.

The area code for Delhi is 011 which need not be dialled if you are calling within the district. Important service numbers are Directory Assistance 199. Complaints, 198. Operator Assisted Trunk Information 183. Assistance 181. Delay inquiry 188. Trunk Bookings 180 (urgent,) and 189 (priority.)

Practical Information

Srinagar's area code is 0194. Agra, 0562. Jaipur, 0141.

Most deluxe five-star and five star hotels have subscriber trunk dialling (STD) facilities from guests' room telephones. For STD Complaints in Delhi, call 3326700.

For direct dialling internationally, these are the international codes from India for the following countries:

Australia - 0061.	Malaysia - 0060.
Austria - 0043.	Netherlands - 0031.
Canada - 001.	New Zealand - 0064.
Denmark - 0045.	Norway - 0047.
West Germany - 0049.	Phillipines - 0063.
Finland - 00358.	Singapore - 0065.
France - 0033.	Spain 0034.
Greece - 0030.	Sweden - 0046.
Israel - 00972.	Switzerland - 0041.
Italy - 0039.	United Kingdom - 0044.
Japan - 0081.	USA - 001.

Five-star deluxe and five-star hotels in Delhi, Agra and the Oberoi Palace, Srinagar offer telex services and a few have facsimile transmission services for guests.

Practical Information

Time

Indian Standard Time (IST) is five and a half hours ahead of Greenwich Mean Time (GMT) and Central European Time. 10 and a half hours ahead of American Eastern Standard Time and four and a half hours behind Australian Eastern Standard Time.

Tipping

Tipping is expected (10 per cent) at restaurants and hotels where service charges are not included in the bill. More so than perhaps in any other country of Asia, tipping is expected from young boys who will fight themselves and you to lump your bags at an airport to a train conductor who will miraculously discover an empty seat on a train that has been booked out for weeks ahead. The tip given to the man who watches your shoes at temples and mosques is his livelihood. Tips are expected everywhere by anyone who performs a service. It at your discretion whether you tip taxi drivers.

Lake Nagin, Houseboat Flic

Practical Information

Tourist Services

Government of India Tourist Office, 88 Janpath. Tel: 3320005, 3320342. Closed Sunday. New Delhi Domestic Airport. Tel: 391196. Indiri Gandhi International Airport. Tel: 391315. Open 24 hours.

India Tourist Development Corporation (ITDC), L-Block, Connaught Place. Tel: 350331, 352336.
Offices are also at the following ITDC hotels:

Hotel Ashok (Tel: 600121;)
Hotel Janpath (Tel. 350070;)
Hotel Lodhi (Tel:619422;)
Hotel Ranjit (Tel: 266001;)
Hotel Kanishka (Tel: 343400;)
Hotel Samrat (Tel: 603030;)
Hotel Ashok Yatri Niwas (Tel: 344511)
Indira Gandhi International Airport. Tel: 392825.

Delhi Tourism Development Corporation, N-Block, Connaught Place. Tel: 331363.

DTDC also has offices or information counters at the following:
Moolchand Office Complex. Tel: 615025
New Delhi Railway Station. Tel: 321078
Nizamuddin Railway Station. Tel: 611712
Interstate Bus Terminus. Tel: 227555
Delhi Emporium. Tel: 343287
Indira Gandhi International Airport (open 24 hours.)
Tel: 391213

State Government Tourist Offices

Andaman and Nicobar Islands, 4-105, Curzon Road Hostel, Kausturba Gandhi Marg. Tel: 387015.
Andhra Pradesh, Andhra Bhawan, Ashoka Rd.
Tel: 382031.
Arunachal Pradesh, Arunchal Bhawan, Kautilya Marg, Chanakyapuri. Tel: 3013915.
Assam, B-1, Baba Kharak Singh Marg. Tel: 343961.
Bihar, A-5, Baba Kharak Singh Marg. Tel: 311087.
Goa, Goa Sedan, 18 Amrita Shergill Marg. Tel: 622562.
Gujarat, A-6, Baba Kharak Singh Marg. Tel: 352107.
Harayana, Chanderlok Building, 36 Janpath.
Tel: 3324911.
Himachal Pradesh, Chanderlok Building, 36 Janpath.
Tel: 3325320.

Practical Information

Jammu and Kashmir, 202 Kanishka Shopping Plaza, 19, Ashok Rd. Tel: 3325373.
Karnataka, C-4, Baba Kharak Singh Marg. Tel: 3438662.
Kerala, 219, Kanishka Shopping Plaza, 19 Ashok Rd. Tel: 3323424.
Madhya Pradesh, Kanishka Shopping Plaza, 19 Ashok Rd. Tel: 3321187.
Maharashtra, A-8 Baba Kharak Singh Marg. Tel: 343281.
Manipur, C-7, Baba Kharak Singh Marg. Tel: 343497.
Meghalaya, 9 Aurangzeb Rd. Tel: 3014417.
Mizoram, Circular Rd. Tel: 3017017.
Nagaland, 29 Aurangzeb Rd. Tel: 3015638.
Orissa, B-4, Baba Kharak Singh Marg. Tel: 344580.
Pondicherry, F-Block, 407 Kasturba Gandhi Marg Hostel. Tel: 387486.
Punjab, C-6, Baba Kharak Singh Marg. Tel: 387535.
Rajasthan, Chanderlok Building, 36 Janpath. Tel: 3322332.
Sikkim, Hotel Janpath. Tel: 3324589.
Tamil Nadu, C-1, Baba Kharak Singh Marg. Tel: 343913.
Tripura, Tripura Bhawan, Kautilya Marg, Chanakyapuri. Tel: 3015157.
Uttar Pradesh, Chanderlok Building, 36 Janpath. Tel: 3321068.
West Bengal, A-2, Baba Kharak Singh Marg. Tel: 353840.

Outside India, the Government of India Tourist Office maintains offices in many countries and can provide the prospective visitor with up to date information.

Australia: 65, Elizabeth St.,Sydney, NSW. Tel: (02) 232 1600, 232 1796.
Austria: 1-E-11 Opernring, 1010, Vienna. Tel: 587 1462.
Canada: 60 Bloor St, West Suite, 1003, Toronto, Ontario. Tel: (416) 962 3787, 962 3788.
France: 8 Boulevard de la Madeleine, 75009, Paris. Tel: 42658386.
Federal Republic of Germany: 77-111 Kaisserstrausse, 6000, Frankfurt. Tel: 235 423, 235 424.
Italy: Via-Albricci 9, Milan, 20122, Tel: 804 952, 805 3506.
Japan: Pearl Building, 9-18, 7-Chome Ginza, Chauo-ku, Tokyo 104. Tel: (03) 571 5062, 63.
Kuwait: P.O. Box 4769, Sadoun Al-Jassim Building, Fahad Al-Salem St., Safat 13048. Tel: 242 6099, 242 6088.
Malaysia: Lot No 203, 2nd Floor, Wisma MPI, Jalan Raja Chaulan 50200, Kuala Lumpur. Tel: 425 285, 425 301.
Singapore: 5th Floor, Podium Block, Ming Court Hotel, Tanglin Rd. Tel: 235 5737.
Sweden: Sveavagen 9-11, 1st Floor, S-III 57, Stockholm.Tel: (08) 215 081, 101187.
Switzerland: 1-3 Rue de Chantepoulet 1201, Geneva. Tel: (022) 321 813.

Practical Information

Thailand: Singapore Airlines Building, 3rd Floor, 62-5 Thaniya Rd., Bangkok. Tel: 235 2585.
United Arab Emirates: Tourist Promotion Office, Post Box 12856 DNATA, Dubai. Tel: 695 398.
United Kingdom: 7 Cork St., London WIX 2 AB.
Tel: (01) 437 3677- 8.
USA: 3550 Wilshire Boulevard, Room 204, Los Angeles, California, 90010. Tel: (213) 380 8855.
Also: 230 North Michigan Ave., Chicago, Illinois, 60601. Tel: (312) 236 6899, 236 7869, 236 7270.
Also: 30 Rockefeller Plaza, Room 15, North Mezzanine, New York, NY 10020. Tel: (212) 586 4901-3.

INFOTIP: As many people speak English, do not hesitate to ask for directions or assistance from fellow passengers who will be friendly and eager to help you.

Palace on wheels

Practical Information

Guide Service for Tourists

Approved tourist guides for local sightseeing in Delhi and major cities can be arranged through the GITOs. In Srinagar, J & K Tourism Office will assist and also private operators. These government approved guides hold an identity pass which allows them to enter certain protected historical monuments with their foreign visitors. It is wise to engage only a licensed guide. In most major Indian cities, certificated tourist guides are available to speak English, French, German, Italian, Spanish, Japanese, Arabic and Russian. The fees, modest by most western standards, are based on half day and full day employment, coupled with the number of persons - 1-4, 5-15 and 16-40. The standard charges are for English-speaking guides. Extra may be charged for other foreign-language-speaking guides.

Tours

Half Day

Delhi Tourism Development Corporation conducts the following tours, all departing from N-36 Middle Circle, Connaught Place.

New Delhi. 8.30 a.m. to 1.15 p.m. daily.

Old Delhi. 2.15 p.m. to 5.30 p.m.

Combined evening tour. 6 p.m. onwards on Tuesday, Thursday, Saturday and Sunday.

Museum tour. 8.45 a.m., Sunday only.

Full day

Agra. 6 a.m. to 10 p.m., Tuesday, Thursday, Saturday and Sunday.

India Tourist Development Corporation operates the following tours from hotels Janpath, Lodhi and Ashok.

Half day

New Delhi. 9 a.m. to 2 p.m. daily.

Old Delhi. 2.15 p.m. to 5 p.m. daily.

Practical Information

Full day

Old and New Delhi. 9 a.m. to 5 p.m. daily.

Agra. 6.20 a.m. to 9.30 p.m., daily.

Jaipur. 6.30 a.m. to 10 p.m., daily.

Overnight

Agra. 6.30 a.m. onwards, daily.

Jaipur. 6.30 a.m. onwards, daily.

Travel Agents and Private Tour Operators

American Express, A-Block, Connaught Place.
Tel: 3323946.
Ashok Travel & Tours, Kanishka Shopping Plaza, 19, Ashok Rd. Tel: 3328221.
Also counters at all ITDC hotels and Palam Domestic Airport.
Business & Tourist Service, 212, Surya Kiran, 19 Kasturba Gandhi Marg. Tel: 352357.
Sita World Travels, F-12, Connaught Place. Tel: 3311133.
Students' Travel Information Centre, Hotel Imperial, Janpath. Tel: 3324789.
Thomas Cook, Hotel Imperial, Janpath. Tel: 3322468.
Travel India Bureau, S-13, Green Park Extension Market. Tel: 667433.
Odyssey International, 78, Yashwant Place, Chanakyapuri. Tel: 672415.
Polaris International, 203, Nirmal Tower, 26 Barakhamba Rd. Tel: 46502.
Cox & Kings, Indra Place, Connaught Place. Tel: 320177.
Indian Air Travels, 6-Rajendra Place. Tel: 5719991.
Mackinnons Travel Service, Bank of Baroda Building, 16 Parliament St. Tel: 310840.
Orient Express Co., 70 Janpath. Tel: 322142.
Heritage India Tour & Travels, S-310, Hotel Ambassador. Tel: 690391.

> **INFOTIP:** Keep plenty of small denomination rupee notes. Also, if you photograph people, be prepared to be approached for a tip or suffer abuse.

Practical Information

THE METRIC SYSTEM

Length

1 millimetre	0.04 inches
1 centimetre	0.39 inches
1 metre	1.09 yards
1 kilometre	0.62 mile

Converting kilometres to miles is as simple as multiplying the number of kilometres by 0.62.(e.g. 10km's x 0.62 6.2 miles)

Converting miles to kilometres is done by multyplying the number of miles by 1.61 (e.g. 60mi x 1.61 96.6km's)

Capacity

1 litre	33.92 ounces
	1.06 quart

0.26 gallons

Converting litres to gallons, multiply the num'er of litres by .26 (e.g. 20l x .26 5.2 gallons)

Converting gallons to litres multiply number of gallons by 3.79. (e.g. 10 gal x 3.79 37.9l)

Weight

1 gram 0.04 ounces
1 kilogram 2.2 pounds

Converting kilograms to pounds, multiply number of kilos by 2.2. (e.g. 55 kg x 2.2 121 pounds)

Converting pounds to kilograms, multiply number of pounds by .45. (e.g. 100 pounds x .45 45 kilos)

Area

1 hectare 10000m/sqr or 2.47 acres

Converting hectares to acres, multiply the number of hectares by 2.47 (e.g. 10 ha x 2.47 24.7 acres)

Converting acres to hectares, multiply the number of acres by .41 (e.g. 40 acres x .41 16.4 ha)

Temperature

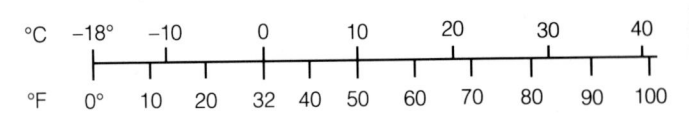

°C	−18°	−10	0	10	20	30	40
°F	0°	10 20	32 40	50	60 70	80	90 100

Practical Information

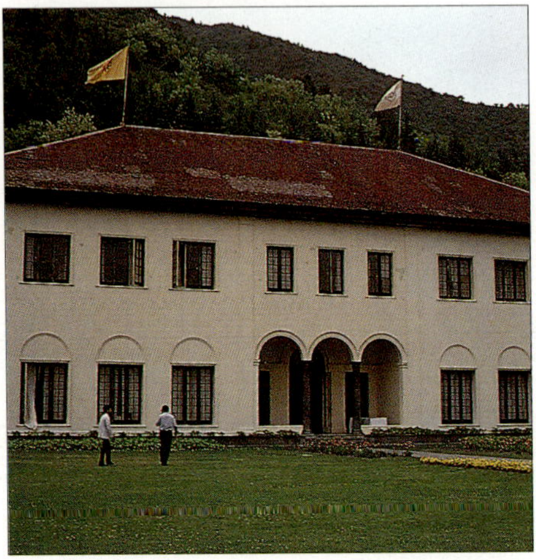

PART V
Business Guide

Red Fort

Business Guide

Contents

Banks
Business Briefing
Business Publications
Business-Trade Organizations
Business Services
Conference Facilities
Credit Cards
Currency Exchange
Import and Export of Currency
Messenger Services
Social Business Associations
Trade Fairs and Exhibitions
Translators

Business Briefing

Main Industries: Textiles, electronic goods, engineering, chemicals, pharmaceuticals, plastics, paper, leather, wood, crude oil, mining products.
Main agricultural products: Rice, wheat, tea, coconut oil, palm oil, coffee, spices.
Main imports: Machinery, fuels and lubricants, iron and steel.
Main exports: Cotton goods, ready-made garments, polished diamonds, gems, jewellery, leather and leather goods, iron ore, tea, coffee, silk, carpet, arts and crafts, perfumes and incense.
Principal trading partners: USA, Japan, West Germany, U.K. Belgium, USSR, Saudi Arabia and France.

Exchange, Import/Export of Currency

There is no import or export of Indian currency allowed. However, this does not apply to rupee travellers' cheques. Foreign banks keep rupee balances with their Indian agents and the procedure is to draw on these balances to issue rupee travellers' cheques to visitors.

There are no restrictions on the amount of foreign currency or travellers' cheques brought into India but a Currency Declaration of amounts exceeding US $1000 carried at the time of arrival will ensure that unspent amounts can be converted back. Exchange of foreign currency other than through authorized banks and money changers is an offence. Visitors trading on the black market risk receiving counterfeit currency.

There is no limit on the import of travellers' letters of credit or travellers' cheques but the amount must not exceed on departure that declared to Customs on arrival. Receipts from banks or moneychangers should be held against departure and reconversion. Foreign currency drafts, irrespective of value, must be declared. The exception of US$1000 applies only to currency notes, bank notes and travellers' cheques.

Should a visitor wish to import specialized equipment or articles other than those listed at the beginning of the Practical Advice for tourists section, application must be made to the Chief Controller of Imports and Exports, Udyog Bhavan, New Delhi. The particulars of each article, the reason for import and the approximate value must be stated.

Foreign and Indian banks open from 10 a.m. to 2 p.m. Monday to Friday and from 10 a.m. to noon Saturdays. A few hotels have 24-hour banks. Travellers' cheques can also be cashed with the cashier in the bigger hotels. A few banks have evening hours, closing on one week day. All banks are closed on national holidays and June 30 and December 31. Making outward payments through the Reserve Bank is frustrating. It is preferable to remit through a draft or mail transfer and keep all receipts.

Banks

Money Changers in Delhi

American Express, A-Block, Connaught Place.
Tel: 3327602.
Bank of America, Hansalaya, Barakhamba Rd.
Tel: 3315101.
Bank of Tokyo, Jeevan Vihar, Parliament St. Tel: 351490.
Banque National de Paris, Hansalaya, Barakhamba Rd.
Tel: 3325015.
Standard Chartered Bank, 17, Parliament St. Tel: 310195.
Citibank Jeevan Bharti Building, 124, Conaught Circus.
Tel: 3311116.
Grindlays Bank, H-10 Connaught Circus. Tel: 3323735.
Hong Kong Bank, ECE House, 28, Kasturba Gandhi Rd.
Tel: 3314355.
Deutsche Bank, Tolstoy House, 15 Tolstoy Marg.
Tel: 3313629.

Business Guide

Indian Banks

Andhra Bank, M35, Connaught Place. Tel: 345536.
State Bank of India, Sansad Marg. Tel:310635.
Also Palam Airport, Tel: 392807.
Union Bank of India, 26-28 D-Block, Connaught Place.
Tel:321071.
Bank of Baroda, Sansad Marg. Tel: 311901.
Indian Overseas Bank, Rohit House, Tolstoy Marg.
Tel: 3319418.
Punjab National Bank, Sansad Marg. Tel: 388148.
United Commercial Bank, Sansad Marg. Tel: 388551.

Credit Cards

American Express, Wenger House, Connaught Place.
Tel: 322868, 344199.
Diners Club, 8 - 3-61 Safdarjang Enclave, New Delhi.
Tel: 609943, 601035, 601301.
VISA, ANZ Grindlays Bank Ltd., 90 Mahatma Gandhi Rd.,
Bombay. Tel: 270007.
Mastercard. In the event of losing Mastercard, call collect
from anywhere in the world 1-314 275 6690.

Business-Trade Organizations

Trade Fair Authority of India, Pragati Bhavan, Pragati
Maidan, New Delhi. Tel: 3318374. Telex: 031-61022,
031-61311. Fax: 91-11-3318142.

Federation of Indian Chambers of Commerce and Industry,
Federation House, Tansen Marg. Tel: 3319251.

Punjab Haryana and Delhi Chambers of Commerce and Industry, PHD House, 4-2 Siri Institutional Area.
Tel: 665425.

Indo - American Chamber of Commerce, PHD House,
4-2 Siri Institutional Area. Tel: 669021.

Indo - French Chamber of Commerce, Philips Building,
9A Connaught Place. Tel: 3327421.

Indo - German Chamber of Commerce, 86 FG Himalaya
House, Kasturba Gandhi Marg. Tel: 3314151.

Indo - Italian Chamber of Commerce, PHD House, 4-2 Siri
Institutional Area. Tel: 665425.

Business Guide

Indo - Polish Chamber of Commerce, Philips Building, 9A Connaught Place. Tel: 3327421.

World Bank, 55 Lodi Estate. Tel: 619496.

Foreigners' Regional Registration Office, 1st Floor, Hans Bhawan, Tilak Bridge, New Delhi. Tel: 3318179.

Special permits for restricted areas. Contact the Under-Secretary, Foreigners' Division, Ministry of Home Affairs, Lok Nayak Bhawan, Khan Market, New Delhi.

Business-Social Organizations

International service clubs such as **Rotary, Lions, Jaycees**, etc., are represented in Delhi. These clubs invariably meet in hotels and it is best to inquire from GITO offices in Delhi and all other major cities for current venues as these can alter from time to time.

Business Publications

Newspapers: The Times of India, The Hindustan Times, The Hindu, The Indian Express, The Telegraph and The Statesman. Also USA Today, International Herald-Tribune, London Daily Telegraph, The Guardian, The Washington Post and the Financial Times.

Magazines: Mainstream, Sunday and India Today. Also The Economic Times, POB 213, Bombay. Tel: 4150271.

Financial Express, Express Towers, Nariman Point, Bombay. Tel: 2022627.
J Journal of Industry and Trade, Ministry of Commerce, Delhi. Also in Delhi are available The Economist, Far Eastern Economic Review, Asia Week, Newsweek, Time, Business World (India), Probe India.

Business Services

Business Centres with secretarial, telex, FAX, telephone and meeting room facilities are localed at the following hotels, (see accommodation guide for addresses and telephone numbers.)

Hotel Ashok - secretarial services, 24-hour telex, teleprinter news service, 24-hour money changing, post and telegraph office, courier service.

Claridges Hotel - business centre, secretarial services.

Hyatt Regency Hotel - business centre with private offices and conference rooms, secretarial service, telex, photocopying, translator and interpreter services and business reference portfolio.

Holiday Inn - business club with telex, secretarial, translation and interpreter services and business library.

Hotel Janpath - teleprinter news service.

Hotel Kanishka - teleprinter news service, photocopying, secretarial services.

Le Meridien Hotel - business centre, telex, secretarial and translation service, photocopying, word processing, electric and electronic typing, 24 hour money exchange.

Nirula's Hotel - telex, photocopying.

Hotel Samrat - 24 hour telex and money changing, secretarial services.

Hotel Siddharth - 24 hour money exchange, teleprinter and secretarial services.

Hotel Sofitel Surya - business centre, telex, secretarial services, photocopying.

Hotel Taj Mahal - business centre, secretarial service, post and telegraph facilities.

Hotel Taj Palace - business centre, 24 hour telex, secretarial services, photocopying and word processing.

The Oberoi Hotel - business centre with 24 hour secretarial, telex, photocopying, dictaphone and word processing facilities.

Hotel Vasant Continental - 24 hour currency exchange, international news teleprinter service, telex, secretarial services.

Hotel Maurya Sheraton - business centre, secretarial, telex, photocopying facilities, dictaphones, offices and board room. Hotel Centaur - secretarial service.

Business Guide

Messenger Service

Express Couriers, 62 Janpath. Tel: 3318071.
DHL World Wide Express, GF-10, Meghdoot, Nehru Place. Tel: 6439460.
Blue Dart, Kanishka Shopping Plaza, Ashok Rd. Tel: 3324175.

Trade Fairs

Delhi is location for many trade fairs but as these vary from time to time, contact your GITO at home for current updates, or the Trade Fair Authority of India, Pragati Bhavan, Pragati Maidan, New Delhi. Tel: 3318374. It organises international fairs and Indian exhibitions.

Translators and Interpreters

These are available through GITO, Delhi. Tel: 3320005, or the Hotels listed in business services, above, offering translators and interpreters.

Conference Facilities

Delhi, Srinagar and **Agra** are all well-equipped for large and small conferences from 10 to 1000 delegates in meeting rooms in from two star to five star deluxe hotels. See accommodation section for capacities and numbers of conference rooms.

Vigyan Bhavan, Maulana Azad Marg. Tel: 384811. Auditorium seats 1500. Simultaneous translation in five languages. Conference halls, committee rooms and offices. Also a large garden.

Indira Gandhi Indoor Stadium. Seats 25,000 persons. Exhibition Complex, Pragati Maidan. Huge facility for international conferences and exhibitions. Inquire, GITO.

Hotel Ashok. Convention hall seats 2500 delegates. Simultaneous translation in six languages. Adjustable stage. All equipment.

Kashmir Sher Kashmir International Conference Centre, Cheshma Shahi. Tel: 72449. Innovative international conference centre with plenary hall, conference and meeting rooms. All facilities.

The Hotel Oberoi Palace and the Hotel Centaur Lakeview, are both equipped to handle conferences.

Air India is a member of the International Congress and Convention Association (ICCA) and its Congresses and Exhibitions Section, with 45 offices in India and 150 in foreign cities, will direct conference organizers to the venue most appropriate, make all arrangements and assist in the planning of any pre and-or post conference tours. There is a wide range of discounts on individual and group airfares for conferences. These may also be appropriate on Indian Airlines internally as IA is also an ICCA member, along with several international standard-hotels.

Major Airlines with offices in Delhi

Many of these offices are situated around or close to Connaught Place or are on Janpath and are open during regular business hours of 10 a.m. to 1 p.m.; 2 p.m. to 5 p.m. Monday to Friday; 10 a.m. to noon Saturday. A few take round-the-clock reservations. Phone to check. Buses for the airport Radial Road 8, Connaught Place, fronting F Block.

Air India, Scindia House, Connaught Place. Tel: 3311225. There is also an office at the Ashok Hotel. Tel: 606669.

Aeroflot, N1 Middle Circle, Connaught Place.
Tel: 3310426, 3312843. Airport: 392331.

Air Canada, 341-D, Hotel Ashok, Chanakyapur.
Tel: 604755. Air France, Scindia House, Connaught Place.
Tel: 3312853. Also at Ashok Hotel. Tel: 606669.

Air Lanka, c/o STIC, Hotel Imperial, Janpath. Tel: 344789.
Alitalia, Surya Kiran Building, 19 Kasturba Gandhi Marg.
Tel: 3311022, 3311019. Airport: 393140.

American Airlines, Care of Nijhawan Travel Service, 78-1, Janpath. Tel: 3329349.

Ariana Afghan Airlines, Surya Kiran Building, 19 Kasturba Gandhi Marg. Tel: 3311432, 3311834. Airport: 391152.

Bangladesh Biman, c/o Jet Air Transportation, N 40 Connaught Place. Tel: 3312119.

British Airways, A 1 Connaught Place. Tel: 343735. Airport: 393111.

Cathay Pacific, Hotel Janpath. Tel: 351286.

Czechoslovak Airlines, 104, Ansal Bhawan, Kasturba Gandhi Marg. Tel: 3311833.

Continental Airlines, STIC Travels, Room 6, Hotel Imperial, Janpath. Tel: 3325559.

Eastern Airlines, Room 6, Hotel Imperial, Janpath. Tel: 3327909.

Egypt Air, Ambassador Hotel, Sujan Singh Park. Tel: 697232. Ext. 512.

Ethiopian Airways, Hotel Janpath. Tel: 351235.

Gulf Air, Hotel Janpath. Tel: 345468. Airport: 394486.

Iberia Airlines, STIC Travel and Tours, Hotel Imperial, Janpath. Tel: 3325559.

Indian Airlines, Kanchenjunga Building, Barakhamba Rd. Tel: 3310071, 3310052. Airport: 391250.

Iran Air, Hotel Ashok, Chanakyapuri. Tel: 604397.

Iraqi Airways, Ansal Bhawan, Kasturba Gandhi Marg. Tel: 3318742.

Japan Airlines, Chanderlok Building, 36 Janpath. Tel: 343130, 343409. Airport: 392185, 392336.

Kenya Airways, Scindia House, Connaught Place. Tel: 3314796, 3318502.

KLM, Prakash Deep, 7 Tolstoy Marg. Tel: 3315833, 3315841. Airport: 393192.

Korean Airlines, 40-42, Pyarelal Building, Janpath. Tel: 353676, 350561.

Kuwait Airways Corporation, Hansalaya Building, Barakhamba Rd. Tel: 3314221. Airport: 393914 (Air India).

LOT Polish Airlines, GSA- STIC Travels & Tours, Hotel Imperial, Janpath. Tel: 344789.

Lufthansa, 56 Janpath. Tel: 343234. Airport: 392283, 393165.

Malaysian Airlines System, STIC Travel & Tours, Room 6, Hotel Imperial, Janpath. Tel: 344789.

Pakistan International Airlines, 102 Kailash Building, 26 Kasturba Gandhi Marg. Tel: 3313161. Airport, 393667.

Business Guide

Pan American World Airways, Chanderlok Building, 36 Janpath. Tel: 351571, 351542. Airport, 393175.

Phillipine Airlines, Jet Air, N 40 Connaught Circus. Tel: 3314979, 331211.

Qantas Airways, Hotel Janpath, Janpath. Tel: 353174, 351434.

Royal Nepal Airlines, 44 Janpath. Tel 320817, 321572. Airport, 393876.

Sabena (Belgian World) Airlines, C 83, imalaya House, Kasturba Gandhi Marg. Tel: 3312928, 3312701.

SAS, A 12 Connaught Place. Tel: 343638. Airport, 393481.

Saudi Arabian Airlines, Hansalaya Building, Barakhamba Rd. Tel: 3310467, 3310465.

Singapore Airlines, Care of Jet Air Transportation, N 40 Connaught Place. Tel: 3314979, 3313221.

India Gate

Business Guide

Swissair, 56 Janpath. Tel: 344386.

Syrian Arab Airlines, 13-90, Connaught Place. Tel: 343218.

Thai International, A 12, Connaught Place. Tel: 343608. Airport, 392526.

Turkish Airways, 56 Janpath. Tel: 3326613. Airport: 394296.

Trans World Airlines, G 56 Connaught Place. Tel: 323718.

Royal Jordanian Airlines, G-56 Connaught Circus. Tel: 3319868.

United Airlines, NK Travel Representations, Central Court Hotel, Connaught Circus. Tel: 3315013.

Vayudoot, Malhotra Building, Janpath. Tel: 3312779.

Delhi Airport, 5452126 ex. 2268. Safdarjung Airport, 623056.

Zambian Airways, c/o Ajanta Travel & Tours, Hotel Janpath. Tel: 312029.

Business Guide

Map

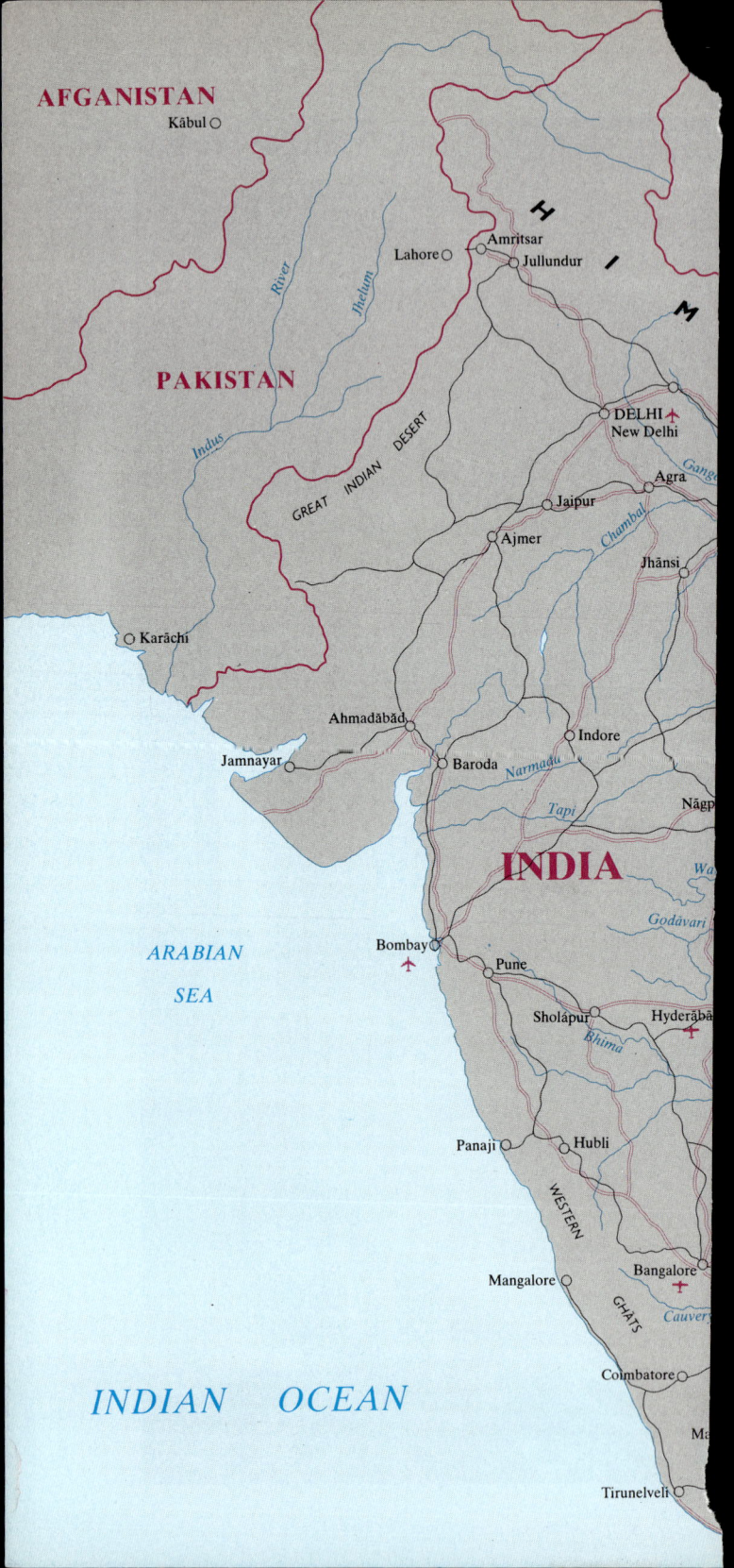

AFGANISTAN
- Kābul

PAKISTAN
- Lahore
- Amritsar
- Jullundur
- Karāchi

Indus River
Jhelum

GREAT INDIAN DESERT

H I M

INDIA
- DELHI
- New Delhi
- Agra
- Jaipur
- Ajmer
- Jhānsi
- Ahmadābād
- Jamnayar
- Baroda
- Indore
- Nāgp
- Bombay
- Pune
- Sholāpur
- Hyderābā
- Panaji
- Hubli
- Mangalore
- Bangalore
- Coimbatore
- Tirunelveli

Gange
Chambal
Narmada
Tapi
Wa
Godāvari
Bhima
Cauver

WESTERN GHATS

ARABIAN SEA

INDIAN OCEAN

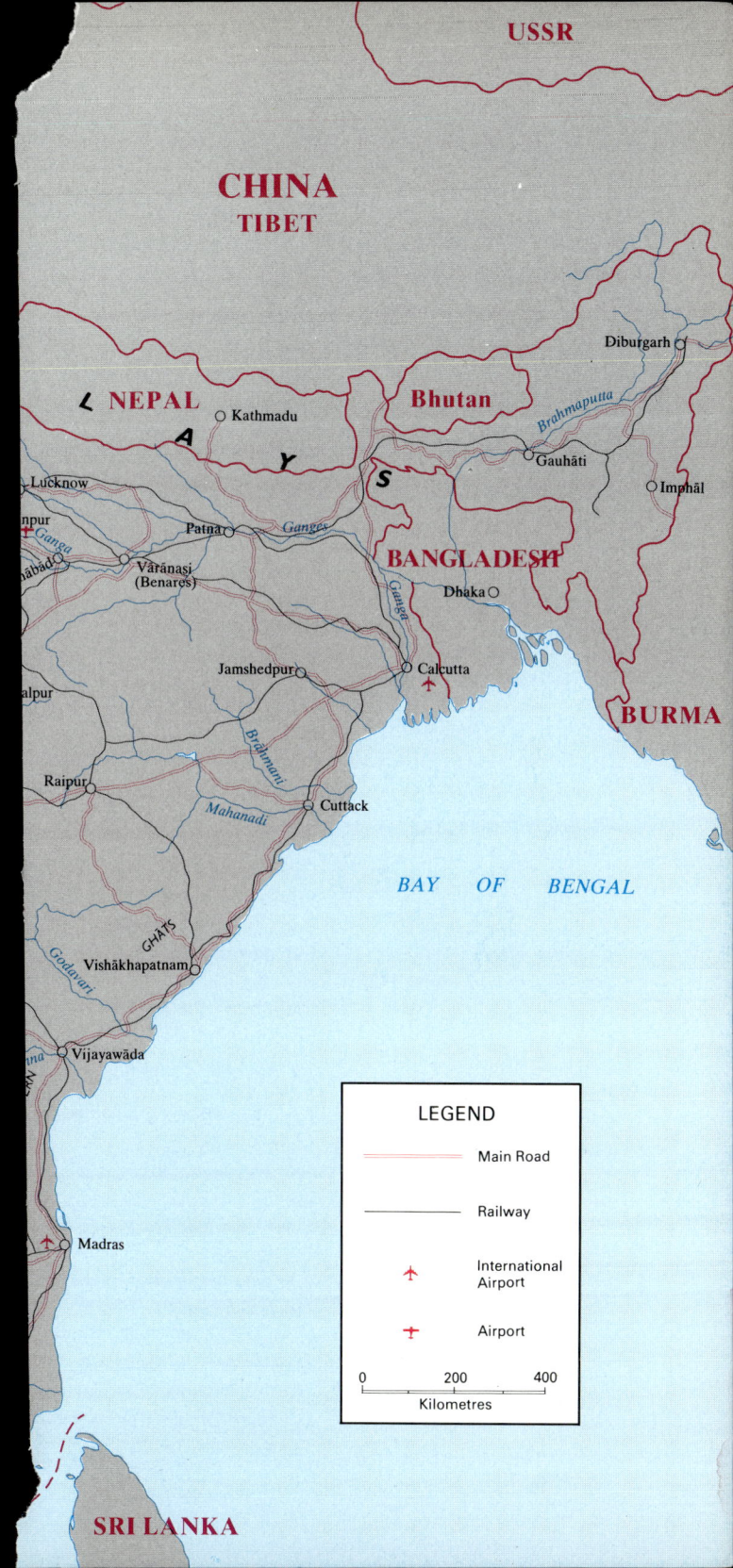

LEGEND

― Main Road
― Railway
✈ International Airport
✈ Airport

0 — 200 — 400 Kilometres

Alphabetical Index

A
A-Z Summary 114
Advance Planning 117
Agra 52, 92
Ahura Mazda 22
Airlines 187
Akbar 26
Alcoholic drinks 152
Anangpal 51
Antiquities 163
Architecture 43
Art Galleries 124
Ashoka 35
Ashoka's Pillar 58, 62
Ashokas Pillar 62
Athletics 164
Aurangzeb 46, 54, 93

B
Babysitting 125
Banks 182
Barbur 26
Bhagirath Palace 57
Black Jews 23
Brahma 20
Buddha 21
Buddhism 20
Business Briefing 181
Business Guide 181
Business Publications 184
Business Services 184

C
Camping 104
Chandni Chowk 53, 57
Cheshma Shahi 87
Children's Entertainment 124
Chola Kingdom 36
Christianity 24
Cinemas 125
Climate 11
Clothing 117
Commerce 16
Conference Facilities 186
Connaught Place 53, 58
Consulates 138
Crafts Museum 65
Crime 142
Currency 122
Customs 120

D
Dance 126
Death 142
Delhi Gate 53, 62
Delhi Sultanate 36
Delhi Zoo 66
Delhi Town Plan 98
Delhi,
  3000 years of History 51
Dhillika 53
Digamber Jain Temple 57
Digamber Jain Lal Mandir 57
Diplomatic Enclave 75
Diwan-i-Khas 54
Documents 117
Drama 126
Dravidians 27
Duty Free Imports 120

E
Education 16
Electricity 123
Embassies 138
Emergencies 140
Emperor Sher Shah 51
Entertainment 124
Entry Regulations 120
Exhibitions 126

F
Fatehpuri Mosque 58
Fatehpursikri 93
Feroz Shah Kotla 62
Ferozabad 51
Festivals 126-130
Flora and Fauna 12
Fort Museums 55

G
Gauri Shanker Temple 57
Gautama 21
Geology and Geography 10
Getting around
  Outside Delhi 132
Getting around Delhi 131
Getting to India 122
Ghias-ud-Din 51
Government 14
Grace of Empires 52

Index

Great Bath 43
Gujarat Coast 40
Gupta Dynasty 36
Guru Nanak 21

H
Hagi Begum 66
Hammans 55
Hari Parbat Fort 88
Harwan 85
Hauz Khas 78
Hazrat Nizamuddin Aulia 67
Hazratbal Mosque 86
Help 138
Hinduism 17
Hindus 34
History and culture 32
Hotels 103
Hotels in Delhi 104
Hotels in Srinagar 110
Humayan's Tomb 66

I
Import/Export of Currency 181
Indian Gate 70
Indian Mutiny 64
Indira Gandhi 41, 56
Indraprastha 51, 65
Indraprastha 65
Indus Valley Civilisation 43
Indus Valley 33
Industry 16
International Dolls Museum 63
Interpreters 186
Iron Pillar 76
Islam 26
Itmad-ud-Daulah's Tomb 93

J
Jahangir 45
Jainism 21
Jama Masjid 56
Jami Masjid 88
Jamuna River 51
Jantar Mantar Observatory 60
Jawaharlal Nehru 40
Jnana Yoga 20
Judaism 23

K
Kabir 21
Kabuli 64
Karma Yoga 20
Kashmir 80
Kashmiri Gate 53
Kashmir shopping 161
Khajurcho 44
Khas-Mahal 54
Khuni Darwaza 64
Konarak 44

L
Laipat Rai Market 57
Lakshmi 20, 62
Lal Bahadar Shastri 56
Languages, Indian 30
Laxshmi Narayan Temple 62
Libraries with books
  in English 143
Lohore Gate 53
Lodi Gardens 51, 68
Lost Property 142

M
Mahabalipuram 44
Mahabtara 65
Mahatma Gandhi 39
Mahatma Gandhi
  Memorial Museum 39, 62
Map 193
Maurya Dynasty 35
Maurya Empire 35
Medical Emergencies 140
Medical tips 118
Meeting People 28
Mohammed 26
Mohandas Karamchand
  Gandhi 39
Mongolo-Dravidians 27
Mother India
  and her Children 9
Motoring 143
Museums 124
Museum of Archaeology 55
Music 126
Musical Instruments 162
Mutiny Memorial 58

N
Nadir Shar 37
Namaste 28
Naseem Bagh (Gardens) 85
National Museum 71
Naubat Khana 54
Nehru Memorial Museum 72
Nightlife 146-159
Nishat Bagh (Gardens) 85

Index

O
Odds and Ends 118
Old Delhi, Defences and Delights 53

P
Palace on Wheels 74, 96
Palika Bazaar 59
Pandit Nehru 41, 72
Pari Mahal 87
Parliment House 71
Parsis 22
Pather Masjid 88
People of India 27
Post Offices 144
Practical Information 114
Publications in English 144
Punjab 21
Purana Quila 65

Q
Quitab Minar 76
Qutab Minar Complex 51, 79
Qutb-ud-din-Aibak 45, 76
Quwwat-ul-Islam Mosque 76

R
Rabies 119
Radio 130
Rail Transport Museum 74
Raj 38
Raj Ghat 61
Raj Path, in its steps 70
Rajiv Gandhi 41
Rashtrapati Bhavan 70, 72
Red Fort 53, 92
Regional & International Restaurants 155
Religions 17
Religious Services in English 145
Rental Vehicles with drivers 143
Replacement of Certain Items 142
Restaurants 146-160

S
Safdarjang's Tomb 68
Sanjay Samadhi 56
Sansad Bhavan 71
Saraswati 20
Scale of Justice 55
Scytho-Dravidians 27
Secretariat Complex 71
Seminars 130
Shah Hamdan Mosque 88
Shah Jahan 51
Shah Jehan 53, 56, 67
Shahjahanabad 46, 51
Shakti 20
Shalimar Bagh (Gardens) 85
Shankracharya Temple 84
Shanti Vuna 56
Sher Mandal 65
Shiva 20
Shopping 160
Shri Pratap Singh Museum 87
Siddhartha 20
Sikhism 21
Social Organisations 184
Son et Lumiere 56
Spectator Sports 165
Sports 164-167
Srinagar Restaurants 160
State of Karnataka 44
State of Pakistan 40
Subhash Chandra Bose 40
Sultan Ala-ud-Din 51
Suncharl Mosque 58

T
Taj Mahal 46, 67, 93
Taj Mahal 93
Taj and Fatehpursikri 92
Tamil Nadu 36
Telegraph 168
Telephone 168
Television 130
Thamjavur 44
Theatre 126
Tibet House 68
Time 170
Tipping 170
Tourist Services 171
Tours 174
Trade Fairs 186
Trade Organisations 183
Travel Agents 175
Tughlakabad 80

V
Vales of Awesome beauty 80
Vardhamana Mahavira 21
Vedus 34
Vigyan Bhavan 70
Vijay Ghat 56
Vishnu 20

Index

W
War Memorial Museum 55
What to bring 117
Y
Yamuna River 52, 92
Z
Zahiruddin,
 Mohammed Babur 36
Zarathusthra 22
Zoroaster 22
Zoroastrianism 22

Notes

Notes